Politics of the European Union
in Bosnia-Herzegovina

Politics of the European Union in Bosnia-Herzegovina

Between Conflict and Democracy

Doğa Ulaş Eralp

LEXINGTON BOOKS
Lanham • Boulder • New York • Toronto • Plymouth, UK

Published by Lexington Books
A wholly owned subsidiary of The Rowman & Littlefield Publishing Group, Inc.
4501 Forbes Boulevard, Suite 200, Lanham, Maryland 20706
www.rowman.com

10 Thornbury Road, Plymouth PL6 7PP, United Kingdom

British Library Cataloguing in Publication Information Available

Library of Congress Cataloging-in-Publication Data

Eralp, Doğa Ulaş, 1978-
Politics of the European Union in Bosnia-Herzegovina : between conflict and democracy / Doğa Ulaş
Eralp.
 p. cm.
Includes bibliographical references and index.
ISBN 978-0-7391-4945-4 (cloth : alk. paper)—ISBN 978-0-7391-4947-8 (electronic)
1. European Union—Bosnia and Hercegovina. 2. Bosnia and Hercegovina—Politics and government—1992– 3. Democratization—Bosnia and Hercegovina. I. Title.
HC240.25.B67E73 2012
341.242'20949742—dc23
2012002171

Printed in the United States of America

Contents

List of Figures

List of Tables

Acknowledgments

This book is the result of years of research and field trips between European capitals and Bosnia-Herzegovina. The original fieldwork was partially funded by the International Peace Research Association Foundation as well as a research grant by the Institute for Conflict Analysis and Resolution of George Mason University. I would like to thank my wife, Elham Atashi, for her unending support and feedback on writing this book; without her this would not be possible.

ONE

Introduction

This book evaluates the effectiveness of the European Union (EU) as an actor responsible for peacebuilding in Bosnia-Herzegovina (BiH). The war in Bosnia-Herzegovina is one of the most tragic incidents of the past twenty years. Between April 1992 and December 1995, the war cost more than 100,000 casualties[1] and 2 million displaced people.[2] The General Framework Agreement for Peace in BiH (GfAP), or the Dayton Peace Agreement (DPA), signed in Paris in December 1995, put an end to the fighting. Fifteen years later, politics in Bosnia remain fragmented along ethnic lines more than ever. The war in Bosnia continues by other means. The international community expects that Bosnia's eventual membership in the European Union will heal the scars of the war in the Bosnian society.

Bosnia-Herzegovina remains politically stagnant. The Dayton system addresses the immediate challenges of postwar, but lacks the capacity to carry the country toward EU membership. The EU's integration strategy for BiH was developed as a response to the deficiencies of the Dayton system. The European Union officials have set up a gradual integration strategy for BiH supported by different crisis management mechanisms. The objective is to build the capacity of state-level institutions to carry out the reforms that are necessary for eventual EU membership. However, the European Union's strategy doesn't seem to be working as Bosnia continues to stagnate at a time when all of its neighbors are already making significant advances on their membership processes. Croatia is set to become a full EU member by 2013, and Serbia is to receive EU

1

candidate status soon. Bosnia, on the other hand, is still stuck in the politics of 1995. This book explores the reasons for Bosnia's stagnation in its pursuit of EU membership and evaluates the European Union's strategy in the country.

Most of the data are gathered from interviews conducted with EU officials in Brussels and Sarajevo, Bosnian politicians and civil society representatives, and various members of the international community between the years 2005 and 2010. This period corresponds to a time when Bosnia-Herzegovina began to backslide in reforms, turning increasingly confrontational. For that reason, the narrative of the book might stand out as pessimistic at times. It is important to keep in mind that there is no single party responsible for the lack of progress in Bosnia; stagnation is a systemic issue and can only be resolved by designing a new EU accession strategy for Bosnia. This book explores possible resolutions and strategies by looking at fundamental building blocks of the EU's involvement in BiH. It suggests ways to align the EU strategy more closely with the present political realities of the country.

CONTENT

The book captures the tools and history of the EU's accession strategy for Bosnia-Herzegovina and the challenges of the Dayton system as two interrelated narratives. Chapters 2 and 3 explore the realities of Bosnian politics and analyze the quality of Bosnian democracy. The challenges of Bosnia's consociational system and the interventionism of the international community are put under the spotlight. These two chapters serve as an attempt to lay out the institutional and political factors behind Bosnia's stagnation. Chapters 4 and 5 follow the EU's involvement in Bosnia since the disintegration of Yugoslavia and assess the development of accession strategy. Chapter 6 combines the two stories together and summarizes a number of factors that affect the effectiveness of the EU as an actor of peacebuilding in Bosnia. Below are the summaries of the chapters.

Chapter 2 discusses the qualities of Bosnian politics. The first section of the chapter assesses the conditions for liberal democracy in BiH by looking into a number of variables, such as the scope of the modern societal networks, strength of the middle class, level of urbanization and commitment to democratic values among the elites, and the role of media.

Bosnian societal networks are structured around family ties and ethnic relations. Participation in civic organizations such as unions and business associations is rare and limited to urban environments. Similarly, the middle class is economically not strong enough to demand change in politics. The middle 60 percent of the society shares only 50 percent of the national wealth. Although this is not a particularly discouraging figure compared to other countries in the Western Balkans, where income distribution is much more imbalanced, it still falls short of making the necessary positive impact on Bosnian politics. A third factor that is essential for sustainable democratization is the level of urbanization in a society. Cosmopolitanism bears fruit in urban spaces where groups with different ethnic and religious backgrounds mix with each other on a daily basis, forming a civic culture that triumphs over ethnic and religious stereotypes. Prewar Sarajevo was one such example of cosmopolitanism in BiH and therefore has been the constant target of ultra-nationalist Serb paramilitaries during its three-year siege. A majority of Bosnian society still lives in rural communities that do not mix with other ethnic communities unless necessary. Ethno-nationalist parties have their strongest support base in the rural constituencies, as was the case during the war. A fourth factor for democratization is the commitment to democratic values among the political elites. Bosnian electoral processes empower the ethno-nationalists. A majority of the Bosnian electorate votes for ethno-nationalist parties. This has been the political reality of Bosnia-Herzegovina since the early nineties. The Dayton Constitution imposed a consociational system that awards ethnic commitment. Thus, political parties that compromise least win in most electoral races. There have been two civic (nonethnic) coalition attempts in the past fifteen years, but none of them succeeded. A fifth factor essential for democratization is the freedom of media. Plurality of opinions represented in the national and local media is critical for consolidation of democracy. The relationship between politics and media has always been problematic in BiH. During the war, the Bosnian media were fragmented across the ethnic lines; the media reform initiated by the international community has brought some structural changes to the broadcast media, but the relationship between media groups and politicians remains extremely strong.

Chapter 3 evaluates the components of Bosnia's consociational system and performance of the international community as an integral part of the system. The main objective of the Dayton System is securing a balanced arrangement between the Bosniaks' demands for a centralized BiH and the Bosnian Serbs' push for maximum autonomy. Annex 4 of the Dayton Peace Agreement serves as the constitution. The Dayton Constitution introduced a consociational system that set up two strong entities and weak state-level institutions that can operate only through compromise between the entities. The second section evaluates the quality of the Bosnian consociationalism through four variables: the formation of grand coalitions, the use of mutual veto, proportionality, and a degree of autonomy. The third section of the chapter discusses the impact of the Office of the High Representative (OHR) on the Bosnian political system. OHR still maintains the nondemocratic Bonn powers to overrule the decisions of the Bosnian politicians that are deemed against the Dayton Peace Agreement. The lingering presence of the OHR for the past fifteen years is quite controversial for it indicates that Bosnian democracy still lacks its own system of checks and balances and is in need of constant international intervention.

Chapter 4 is an overview of the evolution of EU-BiH relations since its independence in 1992. The first section evaluates the EU's performance during the Bosnian war and its aftermath until 1999. The reluctance of the leading European Union countries such as the UK, France, and Germany to take definitive action to end the violent disintegration of Yugoslavia dealt a massive blow to the political credibility of the EU in BiH and the Western Balkans for the years to come. Although representatives from EU member states participated actively in the international mediation efforts to find a negotiated solution to violence and actually produced a number of peace plans, they all failed due to the Europeans' lack of capacity to carry out threats. The Bosnian War revealed the weakness of the EU as a political force, and pushed the Americans to take the lead in ending the war. The EU was excluded from the postwar security framework. Lacking the political will and manpower to take on hard security tasks, the EU assumed the role of facilitating economic reconstruction and social development. When the EU finally decided to become more politically active by 1999, the political future of the Western Balkans was still unclear. At the Zagreb Summit in 2000, the EU clearly declared that the political future of Bosnia and the Western Balkans lay within the EU.

In the following decade, the EU introduced a number of tools and processes aimed at bringing BiH and the Western Balkans closer to each other and thus closer to the Union.

Second section of the chapter focuses on the evolution of the Stabilization and Association Process (SAP) as the framework of the EU strategy in Bosnia. The SAP aims to keep Bosnia-Herzegovina on the integration track while employing the conditionality principle to encourage reforms on different sectors of socioeconomic and political life. The SAP is designed to serve as a policy tool that promotes reforms for the generation of nonethnic politics, the rule of law, and a functioning market economy, and against corruption and organized crime. The SAP is carried out through the European Partnership. This is a process-oriented partnership where Bosnia's progress is evaluated by the European Commission on a regular basis, upon which further priorities and conditions are added or removed. It is a comprehensive tool that lays out lists of political and economic criteria, recognizing the SAP as the main integration framework for BiH. The European Partnership states that the main task of EU integration in Bosnia-Herzegovina is to bring political stability to the country via its association and harmonization with EU legislation. The failed police reform process, on the other hand, demonstrated the SAP might not have the needed muscle to generate agreement among Bosnian politicians. The last section compares the perceptions of strengths and weaknesses of the EU integration policy in BiH through the eyes of Bosnian politicians and EU officials.

Bosnia-Herzegovina has become a testing ground for the newly developed crisis management competencies of the EU. Chapter 5 first describes the EU's political and strategic motivations to develop its crisis management competencies separate from the North Atlantic security structures. From its early days, there has always been a significant conviction among the key members of the European Union that Europe one day has to develop its own security and defense instruments. The EU's clear failure in producing a vigorous political response during the Bosnian War has led to a renewed effort in developing civilian and military crisis management mechanisms. Following the fall of the Milosevic regime in Serbia, the security risks in BiH have significantly diminished, allowing the EU to test its nascent crisis management competencies on the ground. The EU took over the policing (European Union Police Mission-EUPM) and military peacekeeping missions (EUFOR-Althea Mission) from the international community in the first half of the 2000s. The presence of the EUFOR troops on the ground serves as a psychological guarantee by the international community to intervene in the unlikely case of resumption of violence between the ethnicities. The EUPM on the other hand, has been assisting the Bosnian authorities to develop their policing capabilities in their fight against organized crime and widespread corruption. The final section of chapter 5 evaluates how to utilize the post of the European Union Special Representative (EUSR) more efficiently as a body that coordinates the representation of the European Union across its community and second pillar tools.

Chapter 6 concludes the book by discussing a number of factors that influence the effectiveness of the EU as an actor. These factors are the institutional capacity of EU in its engagement in a postconflict society, sense of moral superiority over the applicant countries, disunity of action among the EU members, and enlargement fatigue. The chapter suggests ways to revise the EU's integration strategy in a manner that recognizes the fragmented political reality in BiH to its own benefit and effectively assists the country in moving forward.

Stuck between democracy and conflict, Bosnia-Herzegovina deserves innovative ideas to break free from the chains of the war. This book explores the deficiencies in the approach of the European Union toward Bosnia's dysfunctional Dayton System.

NOTES

1. In January 2010, the Demographic Unit of the Office of the Prosecutor (OTP) of the International Criminal Tribunal for Former Yugoslavia (ICTY) finalized its last estimate of the number of victims in the 1992–1995 war in Bosnia-Herzegovina (BiH). The total number of killed and disappeared people are 104, 732 out of which 68,101 are Bosniaks (3.6 percent of the prewar population), 22, 779 are Serbs (1.7 percent of the prewar population) and 8,858 are Croats (1.2 percent of the prewar population). There are also 4,995 people killed or missing that fall under the 'others' category. According to those figures BiH lost 2.4 percent of its prewar population during the three-year war. For further details please see http://www.icty.org/sid/10591.

2. The Office of the United Nations High Commissioner for Refugees (UNHCR) puts the figures of displaced people during the war in Bosnia-Herzegovina to 2.2 million people. Available at http://www.unhcr.org/pages/49e48d766.html.

TWO

Conditions for Liberal Democracy in Bosnia-Herzegovina

In December 2010, Bosnia-Herzegovina (BiH) entered its fifteenth year as a postconflict country. The country has come a long way in the past fifteen years: infrastructure has been rebuilt with the assistance of international donors, and a large portion of the immigrants have moved back to BiH, although some still do face daily difficulties. There is now a new generation of Bosnians who grew up without having witnessed the violence of the war. The mandatory travel visas to the European Union (EU) have been lifted, enabling all citizens holding a Bosnian passport to travel to Western Europe without difficulty. The relations with Serbia are slowly recovering from their low during the war. But the country is still not able to make substantial progress on its accession process to the EU due to its postwar political setup.

This chapter discusses the conditions for liberal democracy in BiH by looking into a number of variables, such as the scope of the modern societal networks, strength of the middle class, level of urbanization, commitment to democratic values among the elites, and role of media.

CONDITIONS FOR LIBERAL DEMOCRACY IN BIH

Electoral democracies are the dominant form of government in contemporary world politics. Today, 59 percent of the world's governments are electoral democracies compared to 41 percent in 1989, the last year of the

7

Cold War.[1] Nevertheless, not all electoral democracies are liberal democracies. The existence of an electorate system is not a guarantor of liberal democracy. In many of these democracies, electoral systems do not fully represent all segments of the society in legislative bodies. There are different paths for the development of liberal democracies.

According to the 'modernization path' approach, the development of democracy in a given society correlates with its level of socioeconomic development and modernization. Lipset (1960)[2] and Cutright (1963) argue that a high per capita income, widespread literacy, and established urban residence are crucial for consolidation of democracy. A strong civil society has been seen by many as necessary for the development of a working liberal democracy (Fukuyama 1992; Shils 1997; Arendt 1972).

The 'structuralist path' approach focuses on changing structures of power as the main driving force behind democratization processes. Barrington Moore (1966) emphasized that the relations between the social classes and the state determine the regime type in different countries. France, England, and the United States had political histories that gave birth to a culture of liberal democracy, whereas the relations between the social classes and the state led to the rise of fascism in Germany and Italy. Moore (1966) argues against making generalizations about the conditions for democratization, since each country is unique in its socioeconomic conditions and political history. Ernest Barker (1942) underlines the need for consensus as the basis of democracy, either in the form of common beliefs in particular fundamentals or in the shape of procedural consensus on the rules of the game. Civic culture has an embedded capacity for empathy and a willingness to participate (Lerner 1958). The structuralist path explains the resilience and development of certain beliefs and psychological attitudes among the citizens as a result of the history of the relationship between the state and the social classes. A functional analysis of informal networks could identify a set of common beliefs that might indicate the way to the development of a culture of democracy. Putnam, in his comparison of the impact of informal networks in Southern and Northern Italy (1993) and later in his analysis of informal US societal networks (2000), utilizes the idea of social capital as a common characteristic of any society. Social capital can be both inclusive (bridging) and exclusive (bonding) (Portes 1998). In an ethnically diverse and transitioning postconflict society, like that in BiH, high levels of bonding social capital can be harmful for the consolidation of democracy; intra-ethnic bonding can provide fertile ground for the resurrection of ethno-nationalist political propaganda (Dowley and Silver 2002).

The 'transition path' focuses on political processes, elite initiatives, and choices. This elite-oriented approach emphasizes that an evolutionary process should take place before consolidation of democracy. Dankwart Rustow (1970) identified four main phases for democracy to take hold. The first phase is national unity, with the majority of the population sharing a common political identity. The second phase is an inconclusive political competition between different political elites. The third phase is the decision stage, where conflicting parties achieve some form of compromise and agree on democratic rules. The fourth phase of the transition paradigm is habituation, where a general acceptance of the democratic rules takes place. Historic-political processes, agency of the political elites, and human initiatives are all essential components of democratization.

All of the above-mentioned paths for democratization identify five conditions for liberal democracy: the extent of urbanization, the scope of the modern societal networks, the strength of the middle class, and commitment to democratic values among the elites. The freedom of the media also matters since it directly bears upon the freedom of expression (Castells 2000). Below is a study of these conditions in Bosnia-Herzegovina.

The Extent of Urban Population

It is not possible to know the exact number of people living in BiH. For the past twenty years, there has been no new census conducted due to ethnic and political tensions. The majority of Bosnia-Herzegovina's population lives in rural areas (the estimated rural population in 2010 is about 2.3 million people in contrast to 2 million living in the cities).[3] Urban space, namely 'the city' is vital for the development of political citizens. Aristotle (1983) defines the individual as a 'political animal'[4] living in polis, the most developed human plurality where the state and individuals exist in harmony as natural phenomena. Following the Aristotelian line of thinking, a politically active citizenry is a natural fact of cities.

According to the findings of the UNDP 2009 National Human Development Report on BiH, 22.3 percent of the urban population belongs to an association, compared to 14.6 percent of the rural population. Traditionally Bosnian cities have provided a tolerant environment where a multiethnic coexistence was able to flourish, but the Bosnian war changed the multiethnic structures of the cities drastically.

As table 2.1 demonstrates, the demographic distribution of Bosnian cities has become more homogenous after the war. A Bosniak majority dominates Sarajevo, and Serbs are now the overwhelming majority in Banja Luka, whereas the city of Mostar is divided in the middle between the Bosniaks and the Croats.

Table 2.1.   Demographic distribution in three biggest cities of Bosnia-Herzegovina

	Banja Luka		Sarajevo		Mostar	
	1991	2006	1991	2002	1991	2008
Serbs	54.6%	92.0%	29.8%	11.2%	19.0%	3.0%
Croats	14.8%	4.0%	6.6%	6.7%	33.8%	44.0%
Bosniaks	14.6%	4.0%	49.2%	79.6%	34.9%	53.0%
Yugoslavs	12.1%		10.7%		10.0%	
Others	3.9%	2.0%	3.6%	2.5%	2.3%	0.0%

Strength of the Middle Class

In terms of income, Bosnia rates as a middle-income country where the gross domestic product (GDP) per capita rated US $8,578 in 2009. The average figure for the EU-27 GDP per capita in 2009 was US $32,845.[5] GDP per capita (PPP) of BiH is about a quarter of the EU-27 average and is five times smaller than the Eurozone average. According to these figures, one expects to see a much smaller number of nongovernmental organizations (NGOs) registered in Bosnia-Herzegovina, but the facts prove the opposite.

Table 2.2 demonstrates that it is not particularly easy to build a positive correlation between the level of GDP per capita and the size of civil society. In countries with GDP over US $10,000 the number of registered NGOs are significantly higher than the rest of the countries in the list. Among the group of countries within the $2,500 to $6,500 GDP bracket, the number of registered NGOs is more or less the same. Bulgaria is an exception since it started benefiting from EU funds much more after becoming a full member in 2007. Among the former Yugoslav countries, BiH stands out to be the one with the highest number of registered NGOs. This might be the result of reliance on international donors in the immediate aftermath of the conflict. The number of registered NGOs

Table 2.2.   Number of registered NGOs in Eastern Europe (data extracted from the USAID NGO Sustainability Index 2009)

Country	Population (July 2011)	GDP per capita 2009	# registered NGOs (2009)	Postconflict
Bosnia-Herzegovina	4,622,163	$ 4,525	12,189	Yes
Poland	38,441,588	$ 11,273	73,000	No
Romania	21,904,551	$ 7,500	62,104	No
Bulgaria	7,093,635	$ 6,423	30,500	No
Macedonia	2,077,328	$ 4,515	9,830	Yes
Albania	2,994,667	$ 3,808	450	No
Kosovo	1,825,632	$ 2,985	5,000	Yes
Serbia	7,310,555	$ 5,872	2,100	Yes
Montenegro	661,807	$ 6,635	4,500	Yes
Croatia	4,483,804	$ 14,222	37,000	Yes

does not necessarily imply a vibrant civil society. A similar study conducted by Sofia Sebastian (2010) confirms that although Bosnia has received substantial financial assistance from multilateral donors for democratization and governance reforms, this support has not resulted in the formation of an active civil society.[6]

According to the World Bank Poverty Index 2010, the middle class (second and third 20 percent) in BiH receives only 27.4 percent of the Gross National Income (GNI), whereas the top 20 percent commands 43.2 percent of the GNI. The figures show that the income share held by the Bosnian middle class cannot sustain the relatively large number of NGOs. The USAID's 2009 NGO Sustainability Index describes financial viability as the most challenging obstacle to overall NGO sustainability. Local support mechanisms are not as strong as desired, and the new EU funding instruments remain a "challenge for NGOs given their relative inexperience and lack of skills compared to large regional and international organizations."[7] Only politically nonthreatening organizations receive local government funding. Bosnia-Herzegovina receives a low score of 3.7 out of 6 (1.0 being the highest score and 7.0 the lowest).[8]

Attempts to strengthen and support the civil society in Bosnia-Herzegovina by the international community can become counter-productive when the core motivation for starting a civil society organization is to receive financial assistance from foreign donors (Sampson 2002). According to assessments done in 2004, these organizations on average spent 57 percent of their time on service provision, 27 percent on advocacy, and 16 percent on other activities.[9]

Scope of Modern Societal Networks

The main distinction between democratic societies and nondemocratic ones is the extent of cross-cutting membership. "Cross-cutting membership in politically relevant associations" (Lipset 1960, 88) and "multiple memberships in potential groups" (Truman 1951, 514) are critical for sustainable democracies. Cross-cutting memberships provide channels for expression of frustration and reconciliation in political and social structures as the main components of stable democracies (Friedrich 1942; Schattschneider 1960; Crick 1964; Dahrendorf 1959; Lijphart 1968). Societies with a democratic tradition thrive on these cross-cutting networks. Societies in which political processes and structures organize around these networks go through an organic transition to liberal democracy (Putnam 1992). In multiethnic societies, membership to civic organizations such as unions, business chambers, or school boards serves to build social trust among its members.

The 2009 UNDP Human Development Report on Bosnia-Herzegovina finds that "BiH's social fabric is characterized by fragmentation and segmentation rather than cohesion and solidarity."[10] The level of membership in formal associations is remarkably low (17.5 percent), and only 10.5 percent of the members describe themselves as active members.[11] Bosnian society maintains strong informal ties at the local community level, bearing upon enduring family relations. Such strong ties are useful, especially when they provide support in times of need. Informal networks employ substantial influence in contexts where the rule of law is not consolidated (Solioz and Dizdarevic 2003).

There is a widespread lack of trust in state institutions in Bosnia-Herzegovina. As a result, the informal networks provide a safety net for individuals.[12] They mediate between different spheres: the private sector and the state, bureaucracy and the market, communities and society (Tönnies 1935). Informal networks dominate economic or political spheres. They are multifaceted and multidimensional with participants with multiple layers of loyalty acting simultaneously in several different spheres of action (Wedel 1998). On a negative note, Sampson characterizes strong affiliation with informal networks as a detrimental influence that "inhibits people from fulfilling their official duties to formal institutions, or prevents organizations from operating in an efficient, transparent way" (2002, 3). Nevertheless, not all informal networks of reciprocity are inherently obtrusive to the development of cross-cutting memberships in formal associations.

The traditional Bosnian informal network, *komsiluk* (neighborliness) is one such inclusive/bridging informal network. *Komsiluk* is a form of reciprocity-oriented informal networking. As part of its Ottoman legacy, Bosnia-Herzegovina had a cosmopolitan culture thriving in its cities, in *mahalas* (quarters), where different ethnic communities existed together without interfering in each other's internal affairs. According to Bieber (2000), aside from the spatial definition of *komsiluk*, within the concept of *mahala*, referring to the condition of being next-door neighbors, it suggested rituals based on a common understanding of reciprocity where mutual obligations to visit and help each other on a regular basis constituted the basis of social exchanges. Bringa (1995) also points out that, beyond the neighborly exchanges, formal visits between the Muslim, Orthodox, and Catholic communities for occasions such as births, deaths, illnesses, and religious festivities were also part of *komsiluk* practiced both in rural areas and cities alike.

Nonetheless, according to Bougarel (1996), *komsiluk* was able to operate only as long as the government guaranteed economic and social stability and, as Sampson (2002) agrees, interest groups and participatory citizenship as such demand strong institutions and effective states, of which none is present in postconflict BiH. Bringa (1995), similarly, argues that *komsiluk* maintains social distance and separateness as parallel opposites. "Each religious community needs the presence of the other in order to construct an ethno-religious identity, since it is mainly through this presence that a person is taught to be aware of his or her own identity" (Bringa 1995,79).

Pickering (2006), looking at the practice of quasi-*komsiluk* in two largely Bosniak dominated multiethnic cities (Sarajevo and Bihac), found that the norm of reciprocity is strongest in multiethnic voluntary organizations, followed by multiethnic workplaces as there is a wider choice of interaction partners, and is least in multiethnic neighborhoods.[13] These findings confirm that informal networks run only through genuine voluntary participation. A minimum level of trust between the members of one society is essential for the development of a genuine voluntary motivation to participate. The war in Bosnia-Herzegovina dealt a massive blow to the level of trust between the ethnic communities that to this day remains remarkably low. 84 percent of Bosnians who are part of an ethnic majority, and similarly 83.6 percent of Bosnians who belong to an ethnic minority in different parts of the country, do not trust others (UNDP 2009 Early Warning Report on BiH).

Commitment to Democratic Values among the Elites

McClosky (1964) sees the commitment to democratic values and rules between the political elite as the key feature for the development of democratic stability. The pace of transition from authoritarian regimes to liberal democracies is more sustainable in cases where moderate representatives of the authoritarian ruling coalition and opposition forces compromise (O'Donnel and Schmitter 1986).[14] The first democratic transition process in Bosnia-Herzegovina took place during the one-year period between the first multiparty elections in November 1990 and October 1991, when the Bosnian central parliament adopted the memorandum on sovereignty, and it failed utterly.

In the midst of a worsening economic default and growing suspicions of an imminent incorporation of parts of the country into an authoritarian-nationalist 'Greater Serbia' ruled by Slobodan Milosevic, Bosnia-Herzegovina held its first free and fair multiparty parliamentary elections on November 18 and 25, 1990. The result was a national assembly dominated by three ethnic parties that had agreed to establish a broad coalition to force the communists out of power (Bideleux and Jeffries 2007). Ethnic parties gained control of 98 seats out of 130 in the lower house of the parliament (House of Citizens), similarly they won 104 seats out of 110 in the upper house (House of Counties). In December 1990, ethnic parties established a non-Communist SDA–SDS–HDZ coalition government and a non-Communist 'collective presidency, with the Bosniak leader Alija Izetbegovic serving as the 'president of the collective presidency' (Bideleux and Jeffries 2007). This broad coalition could not withstand the fast pace of political changes in Yugoslavia. The independence declarations by Croatia and Slovenia on June 25, 1991 put Bosnia-Herzegovina in an uncomfortable position.

The coalition split over the question of whether to remain a part of the Yugoslav Federation now dominated by Serbia (overwhelmingly favored among Serbs) or seek independence like Croatia and Slovenia (overwhelmingly favored among Bosniaks and Croats). Following the Yugoslav Army's campaign against Croatia, President Izetbegovic urged Bosnian citizens not to take part in the act of aggression against Croatia as a sign of solidarity with Croatia (Tus 2001). When the Bosnian parliament adopted a 'memorandum on sovereignty' on October 15, 1991, the Bosnian Serb members of parliament, mainly from the Serb Democratic Party, deserted the central parliament in Sarajevo. The memorandum required the parliament of Bosnia-Herzegovina to choose between full independence or a loose Yugoslav confederation on the condition that it also include Croatia and Slovenia to mitigate Serbian domination. In retaliation to the memorandum, the SDS set up the Assembly of the Serb People of Bosnia-Herzegovina on October 24, 1991, which ended the multiethnic coalition. This Assembly declared the Serbian Republic of Bosnia-Herzegovina on January 9, 1992, which then had become Republika Srpska in August 1992, with its capitol in Pale.

With strong backing of the European Community (EC) and the Badinter Committee that advised the EC on the recognition of the breakaway Yugoslav republics, Bosnia-Herzegovina held its independence referendum on February 29 to March 1, 1992 (Malcolm 1996). The turnout was only 63.4 percent, because most Bosnian Serbs boycotted it. 99.7 percent of the votes cast were in favor of independence (Commission on Security and Cooperation in Europe Report on Bosnian Referendum 1992). Subsequently Bosnia-Herzegovina declared independence on March 3, 1992. The war eventually broke out on April 5, 1992 when the Yugoslav National Army (JNA) tanks surrounded Sarajevo.

Bosnia's second democratization process started after the end of the war in December 1995 and remains incomplete. Bosnia-Herzegovina holds regular elections on a free and fair basis. The Bosnian electorate is split between three ethnic constituencies. Most of the time, winners are the ethnic parties. The results of four of the last five elections indicate that the parties following nationalist propaganda win the elections. The tragic lessons from Bosnia's first failed democratic transition experience did not change the noncompromising attitude of the Bosnian political elite. A spread-out international community led by the Office of the High Representative (OHR) enforces cooperation only with some success among the Bosnian political elite in the State Parliament, Council of Ministers, and Tripartite Presidency. Below is a concise analysis of the previous general elections held in postconflict BiH from 1996 to 2010.

1996 GENERAL ELECTIONS

On June 13–14, 1996, the Peace Implementation Council (PIC) controversially confirmed that the general elections were to be held on September 14, 1996. The Clinton administration was particularly anxious that they should go ahead. It was rumored that the elections were set for September in order to boost the popularity of President Clinton before the November 1996 US presidential elections. Less than a year after the cessation of violence, the timing of the elections was premature. The international community feared that the results of the elections would only confirm the consequences of the war and strengthen ethnic divisions. The final communiqué of the PIC stated that the RS President Karadzic should remove himself from the political scene before the elections. The resignation of Karadzic from the post of the RS Presidency and the nationalist Serbian Democratic Party (SDS) on July 19, 1996, amid political pressures from Milosevic's Belgrade had opened the way for the September 14 elections. After Radovan Karadzic had gone into hiding, the Bosnian Serb leadership was replaced by another hard-line nationalist, Biljana Plavsic. Plavsic, who has been previously open about her racist political convictions, under the pressure of the international community, turned against the supporters of fugitive Karadzic.[15] On June 25, 1996, the chairman of the OSCE unenthusiastically gave his final authorization for elections to take place on September 14. Despite "extremely high risks," he acknowledged, any setback "could heighten political uncertainty and political division even more."[16] Other criticisms were mainly about the lack of progress made on refugee returns, the lack of an independent media, and widespread intimidation of opposition parties.

Election results confirmed the divisions of the war. In Republika Srpska, the Nationalist SDS (Serbian Democratic Party) won 52 percent of the votes in the race for the RS National Assembly and 54 percent of the votes in the race for the BiH assembly. In the Federation, the Bosniak nationalist SDA (Party for Democratic Action) received 54 percent of the votes for the Federation House of Representatives and the BiH Assembly, respectively. The Croat nationalist party HDZ BiH (Croatian Democratic Union of Bosnia-Herzegovina) obtained 25 percent for each. The SDA received 16 percent of the votes in the RS for both Assemblies, cast remotely by internally displaced Bosniaks for their prewar constituencies in the RS territories (Malcolm 1996).

According to the OSCE Monitoring Report of the 1996 elections, fear and need for security in the preelectoral period were the driving factors behind the nationalist victory in the elections. Barely ten months after the war ended the campaign period was marred by limitations in freedom of travel and expression.

1998 ELECTIONS

The 1998 elections marked the beginning of the era of nationalist politicians who chose to collaborate with the international community by attending the meetings and paying lip service to the Dayton Agreement, while keeping up nationalist rhetoric. According to the OSCE's Office for Democratic Institutions and Human Rights (ODIHR)'s report on the 1998 elections, the political environment in which the 1998 elections took place reflected the complicated conditions in place since the war, including the fact that indicted war criminals remained at large. The international community had introduced nondemocratic measures in the electoral process which would not be acceptable in normal electoral situations. A number of candidates were scratched from the party lists for irregularities in which they had no direct involvement, against which there was no sufficient appeals procedure in place, and, moreover, the international community provided training and financial assistance to parties on the basis of their political programs. In pursuing these and some other policies, there was an increased involvement of the electoral authorities in the political process, leading to a perceived politicization of the election authorities.[17]

The 1998 general elections further confirmed the triumph of the ethnonationalist card. The winners of the elections for the three-member Council of Presidency from the Bosniak, Serb, and Croat constituencies were all from nationalist parties. In the Federation, Alija Izetbegovic, from the Nationalist Coalition of SDA and SBiH, received 86.9 percent of the votes cast on the Bosniak ballot, and Ante Jelavic from nationalist HDZ, got 52.9 percent of the votes in the Croat constituency. In the RS, Zivko Radisic—the candidate of the allegedly lesser nationalist coalition Sloga, led by Biljana Plavsic—managed to get 51.3 percent of the votes for the BiH presidency. However, Sloga's defeat in the RS presidential election race, given that the entities rule over the state-level bodies, against the hardline nationalist Nikolas Poplasen, the SDS candidate, who ran his campaign on his firm opposition to refugee returns, proved the difficulty of recreating a multiethnic BiH.[18]

2000 ELECTIONS

The November 11, 2000 elections were a first in Bosnia in the sense that the nationalist parties, SDA, SDS, and HDZ, received less than 50 percent of the votes for the first time in BiH's political history. The coalition among the nonnationalist parties, called the Alliance for Change, had the mandate to establish the government on the state level. The nationalists' loss of votes was not as substantial as it could have been on the entity level. The total votes of the nationalist parties at the entity level added up to 60 percent in the Federation and 55 percent in the RS.[19] In the elections of the Parliamentary Assembly of BiH, the SDP received 27.3 percent, above the 27 percent of the SDA and 19.3 percent of the HDZ. Nevertheless, the distribution of seats in the parliament did not really prove advantageous for the Alliance for Change to make effective governance possible.[20] The Democratic Alliance for Change[21] of the Federation-based parties of different sizes, ideological orientations, and national colorations, cooperated at the state level with parties from Republika Srpska that were both in power and in opposition in that entity.

As a nonnationalist political option, the Alliance was expected to carry out lasting reforms and to prove that implementation of the Dayton Peace Accords might yet produce a viable state. Both the international community and nonnationalist Bosnians expected a lot from the Alliance: the eradication of rampant corruption, economic reforms, jobs, regular pensions and a new relationship with BiH's foreign overseers. The reforms in areas where there was a consensus among the parties, such as enhanced revenue collection and fiscal reforms (for example, the merger of pension funds), or where there was minimum confrontation, like the fulfillment of the conditions for accession to the Council of Europe, or that were perceived as inevitable, as in the case of constitutional reforms and antiterrorist measures after September 11, were completed. As part of the coalition politics on reforms that could cause friction within the Alliance (such as reform of the social services sector, privatization and, above all, economic revival), action was either postponed or abandoned.

2002 ELECTIONS

The 2002 elections were the first to be handled by the Bosnians. The results of the elections, on the other hand, demonstrated the fragility of nonnationalist politics in Bosnia. The Alliance for Change coalition, composed of an uneasy cooperation between different political parties in different levels of governance, failed to get the approval of the Bosnian voters. The certainty of ethno-nationalist politics provided an easier choice. The 55 percent turnout at the polls highlighted the growing apathy of the public toward daily politics; the nationalist parties managed to much more easily mobilize their constituencies to come to the polling stations. The tripartite Bosnian presidency was distributed among the nationalist candidates from each constituent nation. For the Bosniak presidency member, the SDA's Sulejman Tihic received 37.3 percent of the votes, above the 34.8 percent of charismatic Haris Silajdzic, RS's Mirko Sarovic of the SDS won 35.5 percent of the Serbian constituency vote, and Dragan Covic received 61.5 percent of the Croat vote for Croat member. The three major nationalist groups (SDA, SDS, and HDZ) dominated the House of Representatives of Bosnia-Herzegovina, the country's Central Parliament, as well as the Chamber of Representatives of the Federation of Bosnia-Herzegovina and the National Assembly of the Serb Republic. In the State Parliament, the SDA was the winner, with 32.5 percent of the vote and twenty-eight seats reserved for the Federation of Bosnia-Herzegovina; the SDS dominated the election with 36.8 percent of the vote, winning fourteen seats for the Serb Republic. In the Chamber of Representatives of the Federation, the SDA won 33.3 percent of the vote, ahead of the HDZ (17.5 percent). Finally, in the National Assembly of the Serb Republic, the SDS led with 33.5 percent of the vote, followed by the Independent Social Democrats (SNSD), who won 27.4 percent of the vote.[22]

According to the OSCE report, the 2002 general elections marked important progress toward the consolidation of democracy and rule of law under domestic control.[23] These were essentially transitional elections. The adoption of an election law marked a substantial improvement over previous elections, and a further step toward national control of the election process under the rule of law.[24] A significant achievement was the creation of state-level bodies responsible for the elections, although there was continued international membership in several of these.[25]

The international community adjusted its approach, in view of the victory of the nationalists in the elections, to form a 'partnership' approach, which was advocated by Petritsch. The following period saw an imposing High Representative, Paddy Ashdown, over the nationalist coalition between the SDA, SDS, HDZ, and SBiH.[26] The international community was divided between the OHR and the American Embassy. The Americans initially preferred to work with a nonnationalist coalition.[27] High Representative Ashdown, however, wanted to work with BiH politicians with strong mandates rather than with tenuous coalitions even weaker than the Alliance.[28] Indeed, defense reform and a preliminary agreement on police reform passed in both the entity and state-level legislative bodies as a result of Ashdown's assertive policies over the nationalist parties.

2006 ELECTIONS

During the first decade of postconflict politics in Bosnia-Herzegovina, the main players that dominated the political scene were the traditional nationalist parties whose uncompromising politics contributed to the start of the war in 1992. These parties are respectively SDA (Party for Democratic Actions) of the Bosniaks, HDZ (Croats Democratic Union) of the Croats, and SDS (Party of Democratic Socialists) of the Serbs. They remained uncontested until the 2006 elections. The 2006 elections saw a partial transition of power from traditional nationalist parties to neonationalists at the state and entity levels in BiH.[29] The main difference between the traditional nationalists and neonationalists is that the latter believe that the existing Dayton constitutional structure can be challenged.

This change was more obvious in the race for the presidency troika at the state level. For the first time, the traditional nationalists, SDS, HDZ, and SDA, lost their seats in the tripartite presidency. Nebojsa Radmanovic of the SNSD (Independent Social Democrats) won with 53.3 percent of the votes for the Serbs, above the 24.22 percent for the SDS; Zeljko Komsic of the SDP received 39.6 percent of the votes for the Croat seat, above the HDZ with 26.14 percent; Haris Silajdzic of the SBiH received 62.8 percent of the votes for the Bosniak seat, ahead of the 27.5 percent for Sulejman Tihic of the SDA. The traditional nationalist parties managed to maintain their lead in the Federation,[30] whereas the biggest change was observed in the RS.

The SNSD got 46.92 percent of the votes and obtained seven seats, above the SDS, which received 19.46 percent and three seats. Earlier, the international community cheered the SNSD leader Milorad Dodik as the moderate democratic leader of the Serbian entity who would finally end the dictate of the radical Serbian Democratic Party.[31] Once in office, Dodik's political rhetoric became more inflammatory and nationalist than the SDS politicians. During the election campaign in May 2006, following Montenegrin independence from the state union with Serbia, Milorad Dodik mentioned that the RS did not rule out its right for an independence referendum from Bosnia-Herzegovina.[32] In the postelection period, with his opposition to police reform, he managed to draw an unbinding Serbian nationalist profile for himself.[33] In Sarajevo, the return of Haris Silajdzic to the center of political power was no less sensational than that of Dodik. Silajdzic previously served as the foreign minister and the prime minister of the wartime government of Bosnia and was a close associate of Alija Izetbegovic. Campaigning with a neonationalist agenda that called for the complete abolishment of the Serbian entity as a genocidal entity put Silajdzic back into the game. After becoming part of the tripartite Bosnian Presidency, Silajdzic did not cease his naming of the RS as a genocidal state and kept emphasizing the centralization of the country into one entity.[34]

The biggest surprise was the president-elect of the Bosnian Croats for the presidency. Željko Komšić, a Croat member of the multiethnic Social Democrats, gained the presidency seat held for a long time by the Croat nationalist HDZ with the support of the non-Croat votes of the Federation.[35] The defeat of the HDZ was not the defeat of Bosnian Croat nationalism, but it provided a hopeful perspective for healthy pluralism in BiH in case of a constitutional amendment on interethnic cross voting. The OSCE's Office for Democratic Institutions and Human Rights emphasized that the full administration of the electoral process was handled by the Bosnians. Bosnian political institutions are mature enough to conduct free and fair elections without the assistance of the international community.[36]

2010 GENERAL ELECTIONS

Results of the 2010 general elections provided a unique opportunity for Bosnian politicians to show goodwill. After a relatively long period of time the Social Democrat Party (SDP) received the biggest number of votes from the Bosnian electorate at the national level (284,000 votes out of 1400,000 votes cast). Similarly Dodik's Alliance of Independent Social Democrats (SNSD) secured their mandate with a 43 percent in the Republika Srpska. Election results have provided a great opportunity to build a nonnationalist social democratic alliance across BiH, but it might prove difficult to convince Dodik to tone down his nationalist rhetoric and agree on a common democratic transition platform.

The election results in the past fifteen years indicate a strong ethno-nationalist bias in Bosnian politics. The fragmentation of the electorate along ethnic lines makes it difficult to run electoral campaigns on a dem-ocratic reform platform. Executive political power rests at the entity level, limiting the scope of politics at the state level. Politicians run their cam-paigns through their alliances with powerbrokers and dealmakers at the local level. The campaign agendas regarding state-level politics generally lack depth and are characterized by nationalist rhetoric.

Freedom of the Media

The state of media freedoms in BiH is at a much better place than it was at the end of the war. There are, however, a number of challenges in terms of continuing influence of politicians on media bosses. Pluralism is the bedrock of liberal democracy. Plurality of voices expressed in the media is an indication of the extent of liberties in a society. The role of the media is crucial for the creation of the informed citizen and for the devel-opment of liberal democracy. Being 'informed' of different perspectives enables the individual to make choices between the options provided (Jefferson 1789, ME 7:253). Impartiality, pluralism, and freedom of choice, in return, determine the media freedom. Freedom of the media in a multi-ethnic society guarantees free and fair representation of the views of all ethnic and nonethnic groups through the use of all possible media chan-nels without being subjected to political pressure. However, media free-doms also warrant a high degree of self-control and care by media groups so that hate speech and ethnic/religious inflammatory language are avoided at all costs.

The war in Bosnia destroyed its previously integrated information system (Institute for War and Peace Reporting [IWPR] June 1996). In its place, three independent and mutually opposed systems were established. There was no free flow of information, and the distribution and regulation of both the written press and broadcast programming was restricted to ethnic boundaries. None of the essential ingredients for a common media market existed. The international community essentially wanted to build a democratic media that would be free from the influence of the government and party politics, but strong enough to hold government and the justice system accountable.

The international community feared that continuation of inflammatory reporting and use of hate speech could slow down stabilization efforts in BiH. In 1997, the international community had to use military force to stop inflammatory speech by the Radio Television Srpska (RTVS) station. RTVS, broadcasting from two studios, Pale and Banja Luka,[37] launched an aggressive campaign against the international community, reactivating warmongering speech. In September 1997, SFOR, after issuing several warnings to the editors and founder of RTVS, took control over the transmitters and practically terminated the program from studio Pale. According to Ranson (2005), the use of force by the international community turned out to be more effective than all other media and political actions that had been taken. Some criticized the use of force as the use of undemocratic means, which was in contradiction to the goal of achieving a free media (Carpenter 2000). However, the deeply rooted servile behavior toward authorities on the part of all state television stations in BiH placed them in a devoted position toward the then incumbent authorities.

The declaration of the Madrid Peace Implementation Council (PIC) in 1998 laid out the objectives of the media reform:

> (1) the removal of direct party political control from all media; (2) the establishment of a legal and regulatory framework to maintain media standards consistent with Western democratic best practice, ensure media freedom, and raise journalistic and broadcasting standards; and (3) the adoption and full implementation of Western public service standards at all public broadcasters.

The Dayton constitution guarantees the freedom of expression in Bosnia-Herzegovina. In reality, the Bosnian media is controlled by a combination of private ownership, advertising strongmen, elite sources, state pressure, and cultural dominance. In the Federation, there are several media outlets for critical voices and the opposition. However, in the RS, there is a trend toward complete silencing of media, including marginalization by the government through various means (e.g., financial sanctions and various other sorts of pressure, including death threats) (BTI 2010 — Bosnia-Herzegovina Country Report).[38]

The Public Broadcasting Service of BiH (today BHT), the joint public television for all of BiH, started broadcasting in 2002. Bosnian state public television currently operates with relative independence and struggles to find a balance between the diametrically opposed political and ethnic views in BiH. All of the relevant legislation and regulation documents in the public broadcasting system were adopted as a result of pressure from the Office of the High Representative (OHR); on paper, the legislation looks up to date with European standards (Ranson 2005). The Law on Public Broadcasting System and Service set up the structure of the broadcasting system in the country and established a joint legal entity. Bosnia-Herzegovina Public Broadcasting Service is responsible for the infrastructure, international representation, foreign programs, and regulating relations between the three public broadcasting services. A second law, which should regulate the Broadcasting Service, its registration, activities, and organization, was not adopted until September 2005, and only after concession was made upon the request of Bosnian Croats for three channels in the languages of the constituent people, by three production centers in Sarajevo, Banja Luka, and Mostar.[39] Editorial independence of public broadcasters formally exists; the existing rules are supposed to safeguard the independence of editorials.

In 2009 politicians from the RS boycotted the state Public Broadcasting Service (PBS) for several months. Its management was eventually fired, and people allegedly close to RS political structures have been put in the new management. At the state level, the Communications Regulatory Agency (CRA) continues to regulate electronic media, but the appointment of its new management was extensively delayed due to disagreement in the Council of Ministers and the BiH parliament over the nationality of the new director.

The BiH print media, unlike the broadcast media, is not under the scrutiny of the CRA. On legal terms, the print media are self-regulating since there are no formal regulating institutions. Libel and defamation can thus only be mitigated through the court system, which results in an exceptionally high number of court cases.[40] In the Federation, the widely circulated daily papers *Oslobodjenje* and *Avaz* have become involved in the privatization strategy for the Federation's energy sector from opposite ends, each representing a different political side supported by powerful interest groups. Weekly political magazines in the FBiH voice some criticism of corruption and political obstruction, often failing to substantiate their accusations. In the eyes of the public, the biggest critics of different criminal schemes on all sides have been the journalists of the FTV weekly political program "60 Minuta," who are under continuous police protection due to the serious threats they regularly receive (BTI 2010—Bosnia-Herzegovina Country Report).[41]

In the RS, the management and editorial boards of electronic and print media have been filled with people close to the ruling Alliance of Independent Social Democrats (SNSD). As a result, the RS media has become vulnerable to the political influence of the RS government. Those who criticize Dodik and his government of corruption have become continuous targets of Dodik's verbal attacks.[42] Since accusing RS President Dodik and his former government of corruption relating to the construction of the RS government house, the former director of Transparency International (TI) for BiH claims to have been added in Dodik's "black list" of journalists and intellectuals who continuously criticize him. As a result of political pressure and threats, TI closed down its Banja Luka office for a while.

CONCLUSION

This chapter evaluated the conditions for liberal democracy in Bosnia-Herzegovina by looking into different variables such as the scope of modern societal networks, strength of the middle class, level of urbanization, and commitment to democratic values among the elites and the role of media.

Bosnia has its own unique traditions of social cooperation called *komsiluk*, based on coexistence of different ethnic and religious communities under an extra-systemic political authority: Ottoman Empire (Istanbul), Austria-Hungary (Vienna), or Yugoslavia (Belgrade). This social networking model went through upheavals every time the larger extra-systemic political authority disintegrated. Yugoslav Socialism's motto of brotherhood and unity has failed to replace the traditional network with a modern one. The war destroyed what was left of this traditional model.

Despite international assistance on the development of a Bosnian civil society over the past fifteen years, participation rates in civic organizations remain low.

The majority of the Bosnians still live in rural areas and maintain minimum contact with people of other ethnic origins. Traditionally Sarajevo and other cities like Tuzla, Mostar, and Banja Luka have been the cosmopolitan centers of the country where different ethnic groups have intermixed and produced a distinct Bosnian culture. The war has affected the demographic structures of these cities and created societies dominated by one ethnic group. The demise of Bosnian cosmopolitanism has led to the development of three parallel Bosniak, Croat, and Serbian societies in the country with different orientations for the future of BiH.

One of the crucial components for the development of liberal democracy is the presence of a strong middle class. In Bosnia-Herzegovina the economic power of the middle class is not strong enough to become a source of political influence. The income disparity between the top 20 percent and the rest of the society, high unemployment rates among the youth, and the low level of the GDP per capita create a sense of hopelessness about the future of the country. Political apathy is widespread among the society as evidenced in the election participation rates. Under the guidance of the international community Bosnia has built institutions and processes that are essential for democratic regimes. Nevertheless without the push of a strong middle class, the Bosnian political elite continues to appease the electorate by hostile ethno-nationalist language as a card that is guaranteed to triumph. The election results in the past fifteen years indicate that Bosnian politicians do not feel any pressure to adopt a civil and tolerant political discourse. The media freedoms are not lived to the fullest extent due to close ties between politicians and media tycoons, especially in Republika Srpska. During the immediate postconflict period Bosnian media acted as an agent of hate speech and ethnic hatred until the international community intervened. Although Bosnian media is much less hostile now compared to the late nineties, there is still a long way to go in terms of reaching the international standards of journalistic ethics.

The next chapter evaluates the components of the Dayton system and the performance of the international community as the arbiter of this unique consociational system.

NOTES

1. According to the 2011 Report of the Freedom House survey, 115 out of 194 countries are run as electoral democracies. In 1989, 69 out of 167 countries were electoral democracies. The data are available at http://www.freedomhouse.org/images/File/ fiw/historical/ElectoralDemocracyNumbersFIW1989-2011.pdf.

2. Martin Lipset (1960) conducted a quantitative analysis of sixteen socioeconomic variables in a number of countries and concluded that the more well-to-do citizens there are in a given country, the more attempts at democratization should be expected.

3. According to the 2002 report on environment in Bosnia-Herzegovina published by the Civil Society Promotion Center in Sarajevo, it is expected that the urban population will become larger than the rural in 2014 and will reach 2.4 million by 2030. The rural population is expected to decline from 2.3 million in 2005 to 1.6 million in 2030. For further information please see http://enrin.grida.no/htmls/bosnia/bosnia2002/acrobat/Population.pdf.

4. Political animal (politikon zoon) is one, "who lives/whose nature is to live, in a polis (state)"; from *Nichomachean Ethics*, I vii ad fin.

5. The average GDP in the Eurozone was US $38,084 in 2009. The data are available at the World Banks Indicators website: http://databank.worldbank.org/ddp/

6. The FRIDE Report 2010 on Assessing Democracy Assistance in Bosnia.

7. USAID's 2009 NGO Sustainability Index evaluation report on Bosnia-Herzegovina is available at http://www.usaid.gov/locations/europe_eurasia/dem_gov/ngoindex/2009/bosnia_herzegovina.pdf.

8. Score 1.0 corresponds to consolidation of NGOs and score 7.0 corresponds to early transition stage.

9. A survey undertaken by the Independent Bureau of Humanitarian Issues (IBHI) in 2008.

10. The report is available at http://hdr.undp.org/en/reports/nationalreports/europethecis/bosniaherzegovina/name,19714,en.html.

11. Ibid, p. 22

12. According to 2009 UNDP Early Warning Report on BiH, the average support for police was at a low 53 percent and at 48 percent for the judiciary system in November 2009. Results are available at http://www.undp.ba/upload/publications/Early%20Warning%20System%202009.pdf.

13. The low level of *komsiluk* practice might be explained due to the fact that the neighborhood is the least voluntary space where interactions between ethnic groups take place compared to the work place or formal associations.

14. The authoritarian coalitions consist of hard-liners committed to maintaining the authoritarian rule and soft-liners who are willing to negotiate. Opposition forces on the other hand vary from opportunists, former regime supporters, moderates, and prodemocratization forces who still maintain a degree of respect to traditional elites such as the military and church, to radicals who demand major democratic transformation with no compromise.

15. Biljana Plavsic is a former member of the SDS wartime leadership. She was supported by the international community in the 1997 RS general elections to curb the influence of Radovan Karadzic and his notorious SDS party due to her open approval of the Dayton Accords. In 2000, she was indicted for war crimes, surrendered to the ICTY in January 2002, and after pleading guilty to the charges against her, she was

sentenced to serve eleven years of imprisonment by the ICTY in February 2003. The ICTY charges include:

- Two counts of genocide (Article 4 of the Statute of the Tribunal - genocide; and/or, complicity to commit genocide)
- Five counts of crimes against humanity (Article 5 thereof - extermination; murder; persecutions on political, racial, and religious grounds; deportation; alternatively, inhumane acts)
- One count of violations of the laws or customs of war (Article 3 thereof - murder)

The ruling of the ICTY can be found at http://www.icty.org/x/cases/plavsic/tjug/en/pla-tj030227e.pdf.

16. (IHT, 26 June 1996, p. 6).

17. The final report of the Office for Democratic Institutions and Human Rights Bosnia-Herzegovina Elections held September 12–13, 1998, is available at http://www.osce.org/odihr/elections/bih/14045.

18. Results of the 1998 general elections can be reached at http://www.izbori.ba/Documents/Rezultati%20izbora%2096-2002/98results/results98.pdf

19. In the elections for the House of Representatives of the Federation, SDP won 26.1 percent of the votes, while the Bosniak nationalist SDA won 26.8 percent and the Croat nationalist HDZ, 17.5 percent, and another Bosniak nationalist SBiH, 14.9 percent. In the elections in the Republika Srpska, the social democrat coalition, including SNSD, received 10.6 percent, while PDP got 15.2 percent and SDS, 39.7 percent. The Final Results of the General Elections 2000 is available at http://www.izbori.ba/Documents/Rezultati%20izbora%2096-2002/2000gen/400_horfbih.pdf

20. The SDA (Bosniak nationalists) had eight seats, the SDS (Serb nationalists) had six, the HDZ (Croat nationalists) had five, while the SDP (Social Democrat multiethnic) had nine, the SNSD (Serbian independent social democrats) had only one, the PDP (Serbian nationalists) had two, and finally the SBiH (Bosniak nationalists) had five.

21. The member parties of the Alliance were the Social Democratic Party (SDP), the Party for BiH (SBiH), the New Croat Initiative (NHI), the Bosnia-Herzegovina Patriotic Party (BPS), the Republican Party, the Civil Democratic Party (GDS), the Croat Peasant Party (HSS), the Liberal Democratic Party (LDS), the Democratic Party of Pensioners of BiH, and the Party of Pensioners of the Federation of BiH. The Herzegovina-based People's Party of Work for Betterment and the RS-based Party of Independent Social Democrats (SNSD) later attended the Alliance's coordination meetings, but without formally joining the coalition. The two pensioners' parties subsequently merged.

22. For an election analysis of the 2002 BiH general elections, please see http://www.robert-schuman.eu/oee.php?num=34.

23. Although administered by BiH authorities, they took place in a legal context in which ultimate authority still rested with the international community.

24. The Law provided the essential bases for democratic elections, although the system was extremely complex. Provisions of the election law limit voters and candidates by ethnicity for several high offices.

25. The final report on the general elections in Bosnia-Herzegovina on October 5, 2002, is available at http://www.osce.org/odihr/elections/bih/14001.

26. The three nationalist parties took twenty of the forty-two seats: SDA ten; HDZ five; and SDS five. The coalition-ready SBiH and PDP took six and two seats, respectively, making it possible to establish a ruling majority of twenty-eight. The core opposition comprised the SDP (four) and SNSD (three). For details, see the BiH Election Commission website at www.izbori.ba.

27. After the elections, US Ambassador Clifford Bond met with nonnationalist party leaders several times, and he asked them to forge coalitions both at the state and RS levels. Right before the general elections, Bond told journalists, "Nationalists in governments here would not be considered legitimate by European and other partners in the international community. Simply, there would be no trust in dealing with such partners. We are not sure that they would fulfill their declarations about bringing BiH into Europe." "Nacionaliste u vladama ne bi smatrali legitimnim," *Dnevni avaz*, October 3, 2002.

28. See the International Crisis Group's Report titled "Bosnia's Nationalist Governments: Paddy Ashdown and the Paradoxes of State Building" dated July 22, 2003, for more on the processes of government formation after the 2002 elections, which is available at http://www.crisisgroup.org/~/media/Files/europe/Bosnia%20146.pdf.

29. The OSCE final report on 2006 general elections is available at http://www.osce.org/documents/odihr/2007/02/23206_en.pdf.

30. In the BiH Parliament, the SDA got 25.54 percent of the votes and kept its eight seats, over the SBiH which had 22.99 percent of the votes and seven seats; the HDZ obtained 7.99 percent and secured three seats, against 6.10 percent of the other Croat nationalist bloc which had two seats.

31. In 1997 Biljana Plavsic, RS President at the time, chose Dodik as her vice president to distance herself from Karadzic's SDS.

32. For Dodik's comments, please see http://www.axisglobe.com/article.asp?article=924

33. "If we will have to choose between the European Union and the police of Republika Srpska, we will choose the police of Republika Srpska" (See RSPM Milorad Dodik's comments in an interview published on October 31, 2006, available at http://www.bosnia.org.uk/news/news_body.cfm?newsid=2235 His comments were further supported by one official from the SNSD general secretariat in an informal interview conducted in May 2007.

34. Silajdzic's comments following the decision of the International Court of Justice on genocide in Bosnia calls for abolishing the political consequences of genocide, including the self-proclaimed Republika Srpska. Please see http://www.predsjednistvobih.ba/saop/1/Template.aspx?cid=10340,1,1.

35. Nerma Jelacic, Saida Mustajbegovic, Gordana Katana, "Poll Upset for Big Three in Bosnia " Balkan Insight, October 5, 2006. old. balkaninsight .com/en/main/analysis/5202/?tpl.

36. "The October 1st general elections in BiH were the first elections since the 1995 Dayton Agreement to be fully administered by the BiH authorities. The manner in which these elections were conducted was generally in line with international standards for democratic elections, although further efforts are needed, particularly with regard to the vote count. The election campaign was generally calm, but was marked by sharp nationalist rhetoric and occasional inflammatory statements from key election contestants." The OSCE/ODIHR Election Observation Mission Final Report on the BiH General Elections held on October 1, 2006, is available at http://www.osce.org/odihr/elections/bih/14001

37. Under the influence of changes in the Republika Srpska (separation of President Biljana Plavšić from the Pale regime), Studio Banja Luka split away.

38. The interviews conducted with Bosnian journalists on May 2007 painted a bleak picture on freedom of expression, pointing out strong relations between media groups, businesses, and politicians, especially in the Republika Srpska.

39. Bosnian Croats insisted on a separate Croat channel as the only way to protect their linguistic, cultural, and national identity. The BiH Constitutional Court did not find any violation of the so-called vital national interests in the proposed law on PBS, as suggested by the Bosnian Croats. The law on PBS was finally adopted by both houses of the BiH Parliament.

40. Bosnia-Herzegovina was one of the first countries in the Western Balkans to adopt a defamation and libel law—in Republika Srpska in June 2001, and in the Federation of Bosnia-Herzegovina in November 2002. A Freedom of Access to Information Law has also been in place since 2001.

41. In 2004 the TV political magazine *60 Minuta* was awarded the first Award of Journalistic Integrity, given by Transparency International BiH, for contribution regarding media struggle against corruption.

42. Radio Free Europe reported many other examples of Dodik's pressures on representatives of the press and media, including strong, foul language against journalists, including Milijana Kos of Alternative TV (who had questioned the use of a government plane for private purposes) and Nadja Diklic of Dnevni Avaz (who raised doubts as to the origin of Dodik's property wealth).

THREE

The Dayton System

This chapter provides an analysis of the consociational system in Bosnia-Herzegovina. The Dayton Constitution set up two powerful entities and weak state-level institutions for coordination. This arrangement aimed to reduce the political risk of a resumption of hostilities by introducing a balance between the Bosniaks' insistence on forming a unitary BiH centrally governed in Sarajevo and the Bosnian Serbs' persistence for achieving maximum autonomy. This arrangement needs the goodwill of politicians for effective governance at the state level. But it fails to provide the necessary incentives for collaboration.

This chapter first discusses the theoretical underpinnings of consociational systems. Then it analyzes the Dayton system by looking at four key variables: the formation of grand coalitions, the use of mutual veto, proportionality, and a degree of autonomy.

CONSOCIATIONAL DEMOCRACY AS A WAY TO MAINTAIN MULTIETHNIC BOSNIAN SOCIETY

Incompatibility between national disunity/multinationality and democratization has long been an issue for discussion among political thinkers. John Stuart Mill in his "Considerations on Representative Government" (1958) argues that "free institutions are next to impossible in a country made up of different nationalities. Among a people without fellow-feeling, especially if they speak and read different languages, the united public opinion, necessary to the working of representative government

31

do not exist" (230). Rustow (1970) describes democracy as a phenomenon that could be achieved by any country through electoral experience, provided that there is national unity to begin with. National unity, according to Rustow, corresponds to "the vast majority of citizens with no doubt or mental reservations as to which political community they belong to" (1970, 350). Robert Dahl similarly argues that nationality differences within states limit participation for some citizens, thereby curbing the likelihood for a successful polyarchy (1971, 110–111).[1]

Bosnia-Herzegovina is a plural society composed of three different nationalities with very similar languages but of three different religious faiths. Traditionally each nationality maintains its own political space.[2] Furnivall (1956) describes plural societies as those societies in which different segments live side by side but separately within the same political unit. These segments mix with each other but do not integrate. Bosniaks, Croats, and Serbs of BiH have their own political and informal social networks with hardly any cross-cutting memberships, aside from professional environments.[3] A second aspect of plural societies, according to Lijphart (1977), is the relatively higher propensity for the breakdown of democracy. Lijphart foresees three possible solutions to plural societies: assimilation, consociation, and division. Ever since the dissolution of Yugoslavia, Bosnian politics have been in limbo between the Bosnian Serbs' fear of assimilation under the Bosniak majority and Bosniak majority's fear of Serbs' desire to divide BiH. Consociationalism is an arrangement that aims to prevent both assimilation and the division of plural societies through the framework of democracy. Indeed, as Basch (1998) has argued, if there is any risk of ethnic separation in a country, all political institutions must be overtly pluralistic for a democratic state to persist.

A consociational system has two main components: segmented pluralism in social stratification and a concordant democracy. Segmented pluralism is "the organization of social movements, educational and communications systems, voluntary associations, and political parties along the lines of religious and ideological cleavages" (Lorwin 1971, 141). The system should be pluralist in the sense that it recognizes the diversity of religious, socioeconomic, and political affiliations; and be segmented in its institutionalization of most forms of association along politico-religious cleavages. A segmented organization is different from a functional organization. In functional organizations, people associate only in terms of a specific economic or social purpose such as a trade union or business chamber when the organization is formed around skills or industry. A trade union or a chamber of commerce with restrictive membership to religious, ethnic, or ideological affiliation is a segmented organization.

In a concordant democracy, conflict management is done by cooperation and agreement among different elites rather than by competition or majority decision (Lehmbruch 1967). The elites of the different religious and ethnic communities need to agree and cooperate on the overall management of the country. According to Lijphart (1977), consociational democracies are characterized by four elements:

1. The formation of grand coalitions of the political leaders of all segments of plural societies.
2. The mutual veto that enables concurrent majority rules to protect vital minority interests.
3. Proportionality in political representation, civil service appointments, and allocation of public funds.
4. A high degree of autonomy for each segment to run its own internal affairs.

Below is an analysis of Bosnian consociationalism through these four variables.

Formation of Grand Coalitions in BiH

State-level political institutions in BiH are designed to promote the formation of grand coalitions among the three ethnic communities of the country. The three-member Council of Presidency consists of one Bosniak and one Croat, each directly elected from the territory of the Federation, and one Serb directly elected from the territory of the Republika Srpska.[4]

The two houses of the BiH State Parliamentary Assembly are platforms for power-sharing between the constituent peoples. The House of Peoples comprises fifteen Delegates, two-thirds from the Federation (including five Croats and five Bosniaks) and one-third from the Republika Srpska (five Serbs). The designated Croat and Bosniak Delegates from the Federation are selected, respectively, by the Croat and Bosniak Delegates to the House of Peoples of the Federation. Delegates from the Republika Srpska are selected by the National Assembly of the Republika Srpska. Nine members of the House of Peoples comprise a quorum, provided that at least three Bosniak, three Croat, and three Serb Delegates are present. The House of Representatives comprises forty-two members, two-thirds elected from the territory of the Federation, one-third from the territory of the Republika Srpska via direct elections. A majority of all members elected to the House of Representatives comprises a quorum.[5]

Unfortunately, such a system of mutual checks and balances has proven to be an inefficient conflict management mechanism in postconflict BiH for two reasons. First, the state-level bodies are structured on top of the entities, which means that the real power rests within the entity structures. This arrangement works more efficiently in the RS given the more or less ethnically homogenous population, but within the Federation, executive power is further diminished in favor of the ten cantons composed of varying degrees of multiethnicity. Lijphart considers the enhanced involvement of the local politics in the running of the regime as a positive side of consociationalism. He argues that a higher level of democratic accountability and evolution of goodwill politics is possible through this arrangement (1999). Vesting of executive power in the entities makes the evolution of goodwill between entity politicians hostage to manipulation by local crony networks. Political cooperation at the state level is compromised with demands of loyalty by ethnic constituencies in BiH. State-level politics become places for rivalry and strife among Bosnian politicians.

On these two grounds, the Dayton Constitution fails the first condition of consociationalism. In the absence of goodwill politics, the Dayton System is in a constant risk of collapse. The Serbian parties from Republika Srpska appear to hold the state-level government captive and defunct for legislating any reform proposals needed for the EU accession process. For that reason, the international community in BiH, under the leadership of the OHR, feels self-obliged to intervene in order to keep the system running.

Vital National Interest as a Practice of Mutual Veto in BiH

A second element of consociationalism is the mutual veto that enables concurrent majority rules to protect vital minority interests (Lijphart 1977). The mutual veto system can immobilize decision making if used with bad intent. This has proven to be the case in Bosnia so far. The Dayton Constitution includes provisions that guarantee the protection of the vital interests of three constituent peoples (Article IV.3.d).[6] The Constitution suggests the setting up of joint commissions comprised of one

Bosniak, one Croat, and one Serb to review decisions on the state level when a majority of one of the constituent nations voices the violation of its vital interests. The BiH Constitutional Court, whose composition and procedures reflect the consociational motive of the Dayton Constitution (Article VI. 1 and 2)[7] acts as the final arbiter if the joint committee fails to come up with a solution.

The biggest difficulty in the application of vital national interests has been the definition and protection of the principle which, to this date, resurfaces as a form of obstruction in the reform process. The failed constitutional reform process is a perfect example of how an element of consociationalism could cause additional crises among the constituents of the state if there is no consensus on the meaning and scope of the concept. Before 2002, there were two types of constituent people in BiH: Croats and Bosniaks in the Federation, and Serbs in the Republika Srpska. The preamble of the Dayton Constitution recognizes Bosniaks, Croats, and Serbs, along with others, as the three constituent peoples of Bosnia-Herzegovina. Yet Bosniaks and Croats were constituent peoples only within the territories of the federation, whereas they were recognized only as a minority in the RS proper. The same inequality of status existed for the Serbs, who were constituent peoples in the RS but a minority in the Federation. In March 2002, with the intervention of the OHR, parties were asked to bring the entity constitutions in line with the state constitution, making all Bosniaks, Croats, and Serbs constituent peoples in the entire territory of Bosnia-Herzegovina. Article 4 of the Agreement on the Implementation of the Constituent Peoples' Decision of Constitutional Court of Bosnia-Herzegovina of 2002 defines the vital national interests of the constituent peoples as follows:

> Exercise of the rights of constituent peoples to be adequately represented in legislative, executive and judicial bodies, identity of one constituent people, constitutional amendments, organization of public authorities, equal rights of constituent people in the process of decision making, education, religion, language, promotion of culture, tradition and cultural heritage, territorial organization, public information system and other issues treated as of vital national interest if so claimed by two-thirds of one of the caucuses of the constituent peoples in the House of Peoples or Council of Peoples.[8]

An analysis of the failed constitutional reform process in 2006 could outline how vital the phenomenon of national interest is in Bosnian politics.

The European Commission for Democracy through Law, the Venice Commission's Opinion on the Constitutional Situation in Bosnia-Herzegovina, and the Powers of the High Representative published in March 2006[9] defined the use of vital national interest as one of the greatest obstacles to efficient and effective governance in Bosnia. The commission recommended the abolishment of the House of Peoples and moving of the VNI veto to the House of Representatives. Another recommendation was to replace the Council of Presidency with one indirectly elected president who would serve as head of state with a limited mandate, thus concentrating the executive power in the hands of the Council of Ministers. Building on the recommendations of the Venice Commission, a working group was set up, comprising seven political parties from three constituent peoples with the participation of Americans and EU institutions. After one year of negotiations, there was general agreement that the parliament needed to be streamlined and the House of Peoples' mandate to be limited solely to reviewing legislation related to VNI issues as a part of the package agreed upon among five of the seven BiH political parties. The ratification of the package failed by two votes in the state-level House of Representatives due to resistance from Haris Silajdzic, head of the party for Bosnia and Herzegovina, SBiH, on the grounds that they did not weaken the entities as he demanded. In the October 2006 elections, he was elected as the Bosniak representative to the country's presidency. The three main nationalist parties that earlier supported the package, the SDA, the HDZ, and the Serbian Democratic Party, SDS, all lost ground in the elections, strengthening the hands of the rejectionist SBiH and its Serb counterpart, the Alliance of Independent Social Democrats, SNSD. Both parties pursued nationalist rhetoric during their election campaigns, with the SBiH demanding the abolishment of both entities—and the SNSD responding with threats of a referendum on secession.

The Dayton Constitution recognizes the peoples' national interest as superior to the interest of the individual citizen. A BiH citizen is not recognized just as a citizen of BiH, but also, and more importantly, as a member of one of the constituent peoples who have different interests. This definition contradicts the European citizenship model that protects the rights of the person against the state. The above-mentioned Agreement on the Vital National Interest provides an expanded definition of vital national interest that underlines the separateness of the communities in BiH. If the constitutional reform package passed in April 2006, it would have limited the use of the mechanism for the protection of vital national interest to one institution, without necessarily curbing its scope. A real change in the use of vital national interest could be possible through the goodwill of the political leaders of the constituent peoples.

Proportionality in BiH

The third element of consociationalism is proportionality in political representation, civil service appointments, and distribution of public funds. Ideally the proportionality principle enables minorities access to public institutions. In Bosnia-Herzegovina the proportionality principle fully applies only to those citizens belonging to any of the three constituent peoples. Citizens of BiH who fall under the category of "others" have to face discrimination by the Bosnian state. The Bosnian Constitution, in its Preamble, distinguishes between two citizenship categories: "constituent peoples" (Bosniaks, Croats, and Serbs) and "others" (Jews, Roma, and other national minorities together with those who do not declare affiliation with any ethnic group). The House of Peoples of the Parliamentary Assembly (the second chamber) and the Presidency can be composed only of citizens belonging to the three constituent peoples.

When BiH became a member of the Council of Europe in 2002, it agreed to assess its electoral laws within one year. BiH had also ratified the Convention and the Protocols without reservations. In 2008, following the ratification of the Stabilization and Association Agreement (SAA) with the European Union (EU), BiH made a clear commitment to amend the electoral law regarding the members of the House of Peoples of the Parliamentary Assembly and the Presidency which would bring the Bosnian electoral legislation in line with the European Convention on Human Rights and the Council of Europe postaccession commitments within a period of two years.

Sejdic-Finci Case

In 2006, two prominent public figures from the Roma and Jewish community, Dervo Sejdic and Jacob Finci wanted to run for the House of Peoples and the Presidency in the general elections in October 2006.[10] The Bosnian Central Election Commission turned down their applications on the grounds that Mr. Sejdic and Mr. Finci did not belong to any of the constituent peoples category and thus were not eligible to run for a seat in the House of Peoples and the Council of the Presidency. Sejdic and Finci took their cases to the European Court of Human Rights (ECHR) in August 2006. In January 2007, Mr. Finci received a written confirmation of his ineligibility from the Central Election Commission. In February 2009, the court agreed to take the case to the Grand Chamber and the intervention of the Venice Commission as a third party; a public hearing took place in June 2009, and the court delivered its decision that the state of Bosnia-Herzegovina was in direct violation of European Convention's Protocol No. 12, which generally prohibits discrimination. The court also found a violation of article 14 of the European Convention on Human Rights, taken in conjunction with article 3 of protocol No. 1, which protects free elections to the legislature.[11]

The ECHR ruling noted that the Constitution of Bosnia-Herzegovina is an annex of the Dayton Peace Agreement, itself an international treaty. The authority to introduce changes to the constitution was, however, vested in the Parliamentary Assembly of Bosnia-Herzegovina, as a domestic body. The court further argued that the powers of the High Representative did not extend to the State Constitution, which, accordingly, made the state of Bosnia-Herzegovina the responsible party to revise the contested provisions. The ECHR decision acknowledged that the Dayton Constitution is a power-sharing mechanism that brought peace to the country at very fragile political times, but also reiterated the Venice Commission's opinion of March 11, 2005, that suggested mechanisms of power-sharing which did not automatically lead to the total exclusion of representatives of those communities that did not belong to the "constituent peoples."

Segmental Authority

The segmental authority assumes a high degree of autonomy for each segment to run its own internal affairs. This is essential for preventing possible demands for partition by one of the segments (Lijphart 1977). In Bosnia-Herzegovina, the entities are responsible for the regulation, generation, and distribution of finances and services within the entity territories proper. According to the Dayton Constitution the entities have the right to establish special parallel relationships with neighboring states consistent with the sovereignty and territorial integrity of Bosnia-Herzegovina. The entities can maintain civilian law enforcement agencies. Each entity may also enter into agreements with states and international organizations with the consent of the Parliamentary Assembly.[12]

Segmental authority allows the entities to design and manage their own political economic strategies, sometimes in opposition to each other. The broad powers vested in the entities provide entity politicians an opportunity to develop their own economic agenda, including privatization schemes, deciding on infrastructure projects, attracting foreign direct investment in competitive industries, and transportation policies. Some of the economic partnerships are vulnerable to the political motivations of entity politicians. In Republika Srpska, the Serbian and Russian companies are encouraged to benefit from privatization programs in the energy sector and invest in infrastructure projects. RS's most notable trade partners are Russia (23.4 percent), Serbia (21.0 percent), and Italy (8.8 percent).[13] These figures demonstrate that the RS political leadership is following its own political-economic agenda as far as the choice of economic partners goes. The Russian Federation is a strong supporter of RS political autonomy in BiH. As a result, the RS political leadership prefers Russian investment in the energy privatization and investment deals to ensure stronger political support from the Russian authorities. Similarly in the Federation, Turkey and Gulf countries play an increasingly prominent role in the privatization programs. Turkish political support to Sarajevo is essential for Federation politicians to generate employment. The partial sale of BH Airlines to Turkish Airlines in 2008 is a good example.

Segmental authority creates bureaucracies with expensive mechanisms. In all of Bosnia-Herzegovina, there are 155 ministries at different levels of governance. There are nine ministries at the state level. Within the Federation of Bosnia-Herzegovina, there are sixteen ministries at the entity level. The Federation also has ten cantons, each of which has twelve ministries, which makes a total of 120 ministers. There are ten ministries in the Republika Srpska taking the total number to 155. During election periods, political parties promise posts in any of the 155 ministries to their cronies in return for their support. Widespread rumors of cronyism cause a high perception of corruption among all groups of the Bosnian society and resentment toward the consociational system.

The findings in table 3.1 indicate a widespread perception of corruption among the three constituent peoples regardless of the level of governance. Those living in the Bosniak and Croat majority areas have higher perceptions of corruption compared to the citizens living in Serb

Table 3.1.   Those who perceive corruption in BiH institutions (taken from the UNDP EWS 2010 report)

Institutions	Bosniak majority %	Croat majority %	Serb majority %
Presidency of BiH	76.0	84.3	85.0
Parliamentary Assembly of BiH	80.5	94.5	83.3
Council of Ministers of BiH	83.5	94.2	86.2
Parliament of the Federation of BiH	82.6	91.7	87.1
Government of the Federation of BiH	83.5	92.8	86.4
National Assembly of RS	90.7	95.2	81.8
Government of RS	90.5	92.3	82.0
Municipal authorities	86.1	92.8	82.7

majority areas. This is mainly because of the complex governance system in the Federation, where there are more political parties in competition for ministerial posts.

Office of the High Representative and Bonn Powers

The Dayton Agreement (DPA) has set up a Peace Implementation Council (PIC) that oversees and manages the implementation of the Agreement. The PIC comprises fifty-five countries and agencies that support the peace process in many different ways—by assisting it financially, providing troops, or directly running operations in Bosnia-Herzegovina. The London Peace Implementation Conference established the Steering Board of the PIC to work under the chairmanship of the High Representative as the executive arm of the PIC. The Steering Board members include Canada, France, Germany, Italy, Japan, Russia, the United Kingdom, the United States, the presidency of the European Union, the European Commission, and the Organization of the Islamic Conference (OIC), represented by Turkey. The Steering Board provides the Office of the High Representative (OHR) with political guidance.[14] Since the inception of the OHR in late 1995, BiH has had seven high representatives.[15] In Sarajevo, the High Representative chairs weekly meetings of the Ambassadors to BiH from the Steering Board members. In addition, the Steering Board meets at the level of political directors every three months.

The Dayton Agreement set the guidelines for postconflict reconstruction efforts. The Agreement is composed of annexes, each of which regulates one aspect of the postconflict reconstruction process, such as the creation of a united Bosnian Army (Defense Reform), constitution, human rights monitoring and training, police mentoring and monitoring (police reform), etc.[16] Different international organizations fulfill different functions under the coordination of the Office of the High Representative. For instance, until the elections in October 2006, the Organization for Security and Cooperation in Europe (OSCE) was responsible for elections, together with a Provisional Election Commission that it established; the Constitutional Court of Bosnia-Herzegovina still gets three out of its nine members from the European Court of Human Rights; IMF appointed the Central Bank governor for a while; eight of the fourteen former Human Rights Chamber of BiH members were from the Committee of Ministers of the Council of Europe (Ruma 2008).[17] The Office of the High Representative is still the main body observing the implementation of the Peace Accords and the final authority in theatre. The High Representatives have Mission Implementation Plans (MIPs) that assign specific tasks to different organizations as Bosnian politics transform.[18]

The international community's strategy in BiH from the beginning was to control the development of Bosnian democracy. The content of the General Framework Agreement for Peace (GFAP) defines postconflict Bosnia-Herzegovina as a state with a democratic political system that emphasizes the direct involvement of external actors in BiH politics, and sets a detailed political action plan. The Dayton Peace Agreement designated the Office of High Representative with the facilitative powers of monitoring, maintaining close contact, and coordinating the activities of civilian organizations and agencies and periodically reporting on the political process as a way to eventual reconciliation and full domestic ownership of politics (GFAP Annex 4 Article 2.1). The consociational character of the Dayton System requires the intervention of the international community.

Bonn Powers

The results of the 1996 general elections confirmed the segregation of Bosnian society after the war. The international community did not see any possibility of eventual reconciliation among the three constituent nations as long as the extreme nationalists maintained control. OHR's designated facilitator role was not sufficient to transform the country. Bosnia's democratic processes needed to be controlled by the international community to bring moderate politicians to power in subsequent elections.

At the Bonn meeting in 1997, the Peace Implementation Council (PIC) revised Annex 10 of the Dayton Agreement significantly and gave the High Representative the authority to make "binding decisions, as he judges necessary, on the following issues:

1. Timing, location, and chairmanship of meetings of the common institutions;
2. Interim measures to take effect when parties are unable to reach an agreement, which will remain in force until the Presidency or Council of Ministers has adopted a decision consistent with the Peace Agreement on the issue of concern;
3. Other measures to ensure implementation of the Peace Agreement throughout Bosnia-Herzegovina and its Entities, as well as the smooth operation of the common institutions at the state level. Such measures may include actions by the High Representative against persons holding public office or officials who are absent from meetings without reasonable cause or who are found to be in violation of legal commitments made under the Peace Agreement or the terms for its implementation. (Article 11.2)[19]

The decision of the PIC concentrated the legislative, judicial, and executive authority in the hands of the high representative of the international community without any legal accountability to democratically elected Bosnian officials and Bosnian society. The Bonn Powers gave the High Representatives the mandate to influence the practice of democracy in BiH without any democratic oversight.

Initially, the Bonn Powers were instrumental in the development of the competencies of the state-level institutions and the implementation of the Dayton Peace Agreement as planned. In later stages, the focus shifted more toward the promotion and imposition of effective governance. In a number of cases where nationalist politicians failed to come to an agreement among each other on fundamental political reforms, High Representatives intervened and imposed decisions using the Bonn Powers. Each successive High Representative used the Bonn Powers in different frequencies and with different intentions, from implementation of the

DPA to undemocratic management of the country. Below is a review of how each successive High Representative made use of the Bonn Powers.

Performance of the High Representatives

Carlos Westendorp (June 1997–July 1999)

Westendorp interpreted the use of the Bonn Powers mainly to put the most fundamental building blocks of a state together: the identity of a state, the identification of symbols and the integration of the state legislation (such as the citizenship law, the flag, the national anthem, currency, license plates), and the dismissal of local officials who blocked the return of refugees or the aforementioned reforms. Westendorp handed over an average of four impositions a month. In OHR Report to the UNSG #14, covering the period from April to June 1999, Carlos Westendorp appears to have understood the functional influence of the Bonn Powers in BiH politics when used properly:

> Were it not for the powers I was granted at Bonn and Madrid, there would have been almost no progress. Some Bosnian leaders still seem to see the Dayton implementation as a continuation of the war by other means. The proposed downsizing of the SFOR presence will not make things any easier. The High Representative's powers are still indispensable. They should continue to be used without hesitation whenever local institutions and authorities fail to support Dayton or to impede our work to put Bosnia-Herzegovina back on its feet and enable its progress towards European integration.[20]

Wolfgang Petritsch (August 1999–May 2002)

Petritsch used the Bonn Powers more frequently than his predecessor. From 2000 onward, OHR decisions targeted the setting up of new state institutions (i.e., State Border Service) and reforming the socioeconomic environment (reforms on income taxes, privatization, payment systems). The individuals removed from office were no longer primarily community-level officers, but also politicians who were obstructing media and economy reforms and managing privatization deals. In 2001, the OHR used the Bonn Powers to stop the initiative for the creation of a third Croat entity in order to uphold the Dayton Constitution. The Croat member of the BiH Presidency, Ante Jelavic, was removed from office for promoting a separate Croat Entity along the lines of the war-time Croat mini-state inside BiH. At the same time, control of the financial heart of the self-government movement, the Hercegovacka Banka, was transferred to international administration.[21] The interventions of the OHR during Petritsch's term were not only limited to the political sphere. On April 4, 2002, the OHR abruptly suspended all judicial and prosecutorial appointments in BiH except to the BiH and the Entity Constitutional Courts, the BiH Human Rights Chamber, the BiH Court, and all courts in the Brcko District that already had foreign judges in their composition. The idea was to create an "impartial and independent judiciary" that is "essential to the rule of law and reconciliation within Bosnia-Herzegovina."[22]

Paddy Ashdown (June 2002–January 2006)

Paddy Ashdown, former head of the Liberal Party in the UK, who served as the High Representative between May 2002 and February 2006, was one of the most prominent HRs. He managed to maintain the attention of the international community on Bosnia-Herzegovina by making frequent appearances on international media channels. He also was the most interventionist High Representative, imposing an average of ten decisions each month. HR Ashdown used the powers 307 times (June 2002–January 2006): 91 times in 2002, 96 in 2003, 158 times in 2004, 91 times in 2005, and 11 times in January 2006.[23] Ashdown used the Bonn Powers in a number of areas such as defense reform, police reform, taxation reform, and education reform (Lexau 2004).

Ashdown introduced new standards for "political responsibility" with the 2002 dismissal of the fBiH Finance Minister. On June 14, 2002, the FBiH finance minister was removed after he refused to stand down despite allegations of involvement in a procurement scandal. At that time, it was unclear whether Bosnian politicians were accountable to their electorate or to the High Representative who removed elected officials and judged the higher good of the Bosnian public. The reason for removing someone from a public position was no longer limited to obstructionism of the Dayton Peace Agreement. The misuse of public office had become an area of international oversight. This principle was part of the wider activities meant to bring more transparency, accountability, and professionalism into the public sector. In the latter instance, the High Representative acted as a president or head of state more than an international overseer.

The head of BiH's intelligence agency was fired without public presentation of any evidence. As 2003 began, the PIC granted the OHR expanded powers to veto nominees for several posts across a wide range of ministries and agencies. A few weeks later came word that the newly formed European Union Police Mission (EUPM), which had taken over from the UN International Police Task Force (IPTF), would have the power to recommend removals to the OHR. However, many impositions have been relatively routine. Others have served to "split the difference" or "go the extra mile" in finishing off almost-agreements or compromises (interview with an OHR Official on March 2006). These are the so-called "soft impositions." The 2002 constitutional amendments in the RS and fBiH are a good example for soft impositions. The Constitutional Court of BiH gave all three constituent peoples (Bosniaks, Serbs, and Croats) equal rights in both entities by amending a few provisions on which the entity legislators were unable to agree despite extensive political negotiations (Lexau 2004). These changes took place only because BiH political leadership already knew what the hard impositions entailed.

Ashdown's use of the Bonn Powers to impose or amend laws declined over time while removal decisions increased, especially of the ultranationalist SDS (Serb Democratic Party)/PIFWC (Persons Indicted for War Crimes) supporters in 2004. For this reason, Ashdown was criticized by some for playing the "European Raj" in Bosnia with no checks on the use of Bonn Powers (Knaus and Martin 2003). The scope of the Bonn Powers was no longer limited to the violation of DPA, but encompassed daily governance issues, like determining the sales tax, which should in normal conditions be the task of the national government. Ashdown's supporters within the OHR defended his period by claiming that the impositions meant to initiate, encourage, and accelerate reforms, rather than penalize. Nevertheless, good intentions do not alter the fact that Bosnia's governance has been overseen by the international community, for the Bosnians, in spite of the Bosnians. The frequent use of the Bonn Powers further deepened the sovereignty deficit of the country. The OHR legitimized its intervention through coercion and the threat of coercion on a daily basis. It imposed EU standards on a semi-sovereign country that has not been deemed mature enough to govern itself by the international community.

Christian Schwartz-Schilling (February 2006–June 2007)

'Clear failure' could be the correct term that summarizes Christian Schwartz-Schilling's tenure at the Office of the High Representative. The nonintrusive policies of Schwartz-Schilling contributed to the intensification of ethno-nationalist rhetoric following the failure of the constitutional package in April 2006, and led up to the general elections in October. In postconflict societies, regeneration of constructive relations between the former combatants is of grim importance. The election processes and the language used in the elections indicate the normalization of politics in the country (Pugh 2004). Schwartz-Schilling, from his first day in office, emphasized his intention to leave Bosnian politics to Bosnian politicians, indicating that "elections are the crowning moment in any democracy. It was not the preferences of the new High Representative but the choices of the voters of this country that would determine how this country will be governed."[24] On March 16, 2006, in a speech to the OSCE Permanent Council in Vienna, Schwartz-Schilling reiterated his position with regard to the Bonn Powers very clearly:

> I have made it clear that I will use the Bonn Powers without hesitation should this be necessary to maintain peace and stability or to further BiH's cooperation with the ICTY. I have made it equally clear that I will not use the Bonn Powers for anything else. . . The days when OHR micromanaged the political process in BiH by using—or simply by threatening to use—the Bonn Powers are over. . . We are entering an era where if BiH politicians make mistakes, the International Community in general, and the OHR in particular, will not step in to make things right. There are two possible responses to this:
>
> - BiH Political leaders can make mistakes and then blame the IC for doing nothing to minimize the consequences of these mistakes, or
> - they can work more conscientiously to avoid making mistakes. (emphasis added)[25]

In June 2006, the Peace Implementation Council (PIC) decided to initiate the process of phasing out the Office of High Representative. The Political Directors of the Steering Board met in Sarajevo on June 22 and 23, 2006, and announced that the OHR was to be phased out by June 30, 2007.[26] Schwartz-Schilling argued for the transfer of some of the OHR competencies to an expanded EU Special Representative without the Bonn Powers.[27] The final decision was to be made in early 2007, after a careful assessment of the overall situation in BiH before being submitted for the approval of the UN Security Council.[28] Unfortunately, Bosnian politics had by then already started its downward spiral after the rejection of the constitutional package that included partial changes enabling more effective state-level institutions in April 2006. The constitutional reform package was essentially a US-driven initiative supported by the Venice Commission of the Council of Europe. It envisaged the constitutional confirmation of a number of responsibilities exclusively exercised at the state level, for example, defense, intelligence and external security, and the establishment and regulation of a single indirect taxation system. It also introduced a number of shared responsibilities between the state and entities, in particular, taxation, electoral process, judiciary, agriculture, science and technology, environment, and local self-government. Proposals for constitutional amendments included an EU integration clause, according to which, responsibility for negotiating agreements with and undertaking commitments to the EU would be the responsibility of the state, although the entities would recommend and approve in advance such negotiations and agreements. The implementation of agreements and commitments would be a shared responsibility between the state and the entities.[29]

In June 2006, the Montenegrin independence declaration prompted calls for a referendum of independence by then-RS Prime Minister Dodik, which were countered by demands for the abolition of RS as a genocidal state by the Bosniak member of the Council of Presidency Haris Silajdzic in Sarajevo. The demands for special status for the city of Srebrenica came after the ICJ's decision in February 2007 that genocide was committed in Srebrenica and led to a further rash of mutual accusations and insults between the Federation and the RS. Failure of the April 2006 Constitution Package and the resumption of nationalist rhetoric during the election campaign led the PIC Steering Board in February 2007 to declare the postponement of the 'transition' of the OHR to June 20, 2008.[30] In his final report to the UN Secretary General, Schwartz-Schilling revealed his new conviction:

> The highly divisive and occasionally inflammatory rhetoric that characterized the election campaign put my resolve to promote domestic ownership to the test; but it also made it possible to make a realistic assessment of the extent to which the domestic political establishments could take on ever-increasing responsibility for their own country's

affairs. Only by establishing the reality of the situation in BiH did it prove possible to identify the mechanisms that will be required in the future to assist this country in completing its transition from postcommunist and postwar fragility to Euro-Atlantic integration and security.[31]

Miroslav Lajcak (July 2007–March 2009)

Lajcak followed a policy of active engagement in Bosnian politics compared to his predecessor. His first priority when he took the post of the HR was to have BiH sign the Stabilization and Association Agreement (SAA) the European Union. According to Lajcak, the biggest obstacle was the lack of goodwill among Bosnian politicians to build consensus for the necessary reforms. The most important was the police reform that required the unification of the Federation and RS Police under one roof. Rather than using the threat of the Bonn Powers, he tried to create neutral platforms on which politicians from the RS and the Federation could discuss their differences on the implementation of the demanded police reform and try to find common ground.

Lajcak embraced the role of an honest broker, promising the Bosnian politicians that he could convince the European Commission to move forward with the SAA once there was a show of goodwill by the politicians. Another tactic he used during this process was to underline the approaching deadline for an agreement. He associated himself with the EU integration prospect of BiH very clearly in his press declarations and public appearances. Lajcak began to promote the signing of the SAA as the only panacea against nationalist politics.

As the representative of the international community, Lajcak managed to give a clear signal to Bosnian politicians that it was their last chance if they were sincere about taking BiH into EU. A last minute deal among the Bosnian politicians known as the Mostar Declaration, which outlined the basic features of the future Bosnian police structures, was considered satisfactory by the European Commission and received confirmation from the EU that BiH could now sign the SAA. The international community hailed the agreement as a success and a turning point for BiH. However, during the months that followed, Bosnian politics remained as antagonistic as ever.

Lajcak's policy of active engagement did not bring the much needed impetus for European reforms for two reasons. First, the international community's attention on the Western Balkans shifted to the handling of the final status negotiations of Kosovo during this period. As a result, the international community did not exert substantial pressure on Bosnian politicians to implement the reforms. Second, Lajcak predicted the positive impact of the signing of the SAA on Bosnian politics too optimistically. His "take it or leave it" rhetoric became less productive once the Bosnian politicians realized that the European Commission is not interested in the implementation of the reforms but on occasional gestures of goodwill for reforms. After endless meetings with Bosnian politicians over compromise on the implementation of the police reform, the reform initiative silently died as the country entered the local elections process in 2008.

HR Lajcak did not use the Bonn Powers to remove nationalist leaders from office even at the height of the heated nationalist political debate between Bosniak Member of the Presidency Haris Slajdzic and RS Prime Minister Milorad Dodik. He wanted to demonstrate that it was the responsibility of the Bosnian politicians to handle their own problems. Lajcak only took action in matters directly related to the obstruction of the implementation of the Dayton Peace Agreement, such as the removal of Predrag Čeranić, a member of the Intelligence and Security Agency of Bosnia-Herzegovina, on suspicion of providing material support to indicted war criminals.[32]

Valentin Inzko (April 2009–Present)

Under Inzko, the OHR is increasingly becoming an irrelevant actor. The members of the Peace Implementation Committee (PIC) are not anonymously backing the decisions of the HR. The EU-US Summit held at the Butmir Camp Airbase outside Sarajevo in December 2009 asked the participation of Inzko only as the EU Special Representative and excluded OHR policy makers from the constitution reform proposal. The Butmir process failed as Bosnian politicians were not pressed hard to implement reforms. The ongoing discussions on a possible deadline for the closure of the OHR and constant postponement of that decision make the OHR a lame duck in Bosnian politics. In September 2009, Inzko introduced eight laws regarding the regulation of electric transmission lines in the Brcko District. The imposed legislation aimed to transfer the authority of the regulation of the Brcko electric distribution system to state-level in line with the EU standards. The RS government refused to implement the imposed decisions and further threatened the removal of Serb representatives from the legislative and executive state-level institutions.

Future of the OHR

The Dayton Agreement designated the High Representative as the final arbiter in cases of conflict between the entities and the state. The DPA does not bestow such political authority to any of the domestic institutions. Annex X of the DPA and Bonn Powers provides guidelines to the HR to exercise this authority. The PIC Conference in Bonn stated that the High Representative can take "interim measures to take effect when parties are unable to reach agreement" in order to "facilitate the resolution of difficulties by making binding decisions, as he judges necessary." Only the High Representative has the right of disposal to determine when to use the Bonn Powers.

As indicated in table 3.2, High Representatives resorted to the use of the Bonn Powers more than 900 times since 1997. There are seven areas of intervention, which can be grouped in two subcategories of statebuilding and peacebuilding. A majority of the HR decisions concerns statebuilding matters, relating to *State Symbols and State-Level Matters and Constitutional Issues* (114 times), decisions in the *Economic Field* (97 times), decisions in *the Field of Judicial Reform* (182 times), decisions relating to *the Federation, Mostar, and Herzegovina-Neretva Canton* (77 times), and *Removals and Suspensions from Office* (191 times). The remaining decisions are related to peacebuilding matters such as the decisions on *Media Restructuring* preventing hate speech (18 times), decisions in the field of *Property Laws, Return of Displaced Persons and Refugees and Reconciliation* that facilitate the reintegration of the society (120 times), and decisions relating to *individuals indicted for war crimes in the former Yugoslavia* (115 times).

The Office of the High Representative has become an integral part of the political system in Bosnia-Herzegovina. Decisions summarized above suggest that the main task of the OHR over the years has been strengthening the state-level institutions at the expense of the entities. The long-term political stability of the country has been deemed possible only through the strengthening of these state-level institutions. Especially during the term of Paddy Ashdown as the HR, the Bonn Powers were extensively used, removing elected officials from power and introducing economic measures in order to diminish the power of entity politicians in the country.

Table 3.2. Decisions imposed by the high representatives between 1997 and 2011

Decisions	Total	2011	2010	2009	2008	2007	2006	2005	2004	2003	2002	2001	2000	1999	1998	1997
State symbols and state-level matters and constitutional issues	114	2	1	9	0	5	1	18	12	14	28	3	7	7	6	1
Economic field	97	2	0	0	3	3	10	3	6	11	15	5	29	2	8	0
Judicial reform	182	0	0	5	1	11	16	30	30	31	44	7	4	3	0	0
The Federation, Mostar and Herzegovina Cantons	77	0	1	5	0	3	2	1	19	4	30	2	1	5	4	0
Renewals and suspensions from office	191	1	6	9	2	3	22	34	6	7	21	14	28	32	6	0
Media restructuring decisions by the HR	18	0	0	0	0	0	0	0	0	0	5	3	5	3	2	0
Property laws, return of displaced persons and refugees and reconciliation	120	1	0	1	3	11	6	4	0	11	10	20	12	38	3	0
Individuals indicted for war crimes in the former Yugoslavia	115	3	2	2	3	1	0	1	85	18	0	0	0	0	0	0
Total	914	9	10	31	12	37	57	91	158	96	153	54	86	90	29	1

Following the end of Ashdown's term in January 2006, the international community preferred High Representatives who were less aggressive political figures, like Schwartz-Schilling. The plain aimed to strengthen the role of the Peace Implementation Council in the decision making of the OHR, allowing for a deeper consultative process between the members of the Steering Board. Bosnian politicians were allowed to act more freely and encouraged to enact reforms necessary for Bosnia's EU integration on their own. The international community wanted to mark the end of the 'Dayton Era,' the end of the interventionism, and the beginning of the 'Brussels Era,' during which the international community's position would be reduced to supporting Bosnian politicians in their efforts for integration into the Euro-Atlantic bodies.

The final decision for the eventual transition would be made depending on the completion of five objectives and two conditions by that date.

The five objectives are:

> (1) acceptable and sustainable resolution of the issue of apportionment of property between State and other levels of government, (2) acceptable and sustainable resolution of defense property, (3) completion of the Brcko Final Award, (4) fiscal sustainability (promoted through an agreement on a permanent ITA co-efficient methodology and establishment of a National Fiscal Council), (5) entrenchment of the rule of law(demonstrated through Adoption of National War Crimes Strategy, passage of Law on Aliens and Asylum, and adoption of National Justice Sector Reform Strategy).

The two conditions are:

> (1) signing of the Stabilization and Association Agreement with the European Union, and
> (2) a positive assessment of the situation in the country by the Steering Board based on full compliance with the Dayton Peace Agreement.

BiH has completed most of the 5+2 criteria required for the transition of the OHR, but the issues of apportionment of property between state and other levels of government and acceptable and sustainable resolution of defense property remain incomplete. And it is unclear whether the fulfillment of the 5+2 criteria would necessarily mean that the state of Bosnia-Herzegovina has developed its own competencies to run the country. There is an obvious unease among the Bosniak policy circles in Sarajevo that Bosnia-Herzegovina will disintegrate once the OHR closes down (VPI Policy Analysis April 2011).[33] The Serb political leadership in Banja

Luka, on the other hand, demands the immediate dissolution of the OHR regardless of the fulfillment of the 5+2 criteria.

Bosniak politicians in Sarajevo see the OHR as a valuable ally, an important deterrent against the increasingly antagonistic political rhetoric from Banja Luka. On the other hand, the RS leadership headed by RS President Milorad Dodik considers the OHR as a tool of Sarajevo that constantly punishes Banja Luka and diminishes the sovereignty of the entity. The debate on the closure of the OHR reflects the paradox of the international community. On one side are those who support a policy of disengagement from Bosnia-Herzegovina, citing that the presence of the interventionist policies of the international community in the past fifteen years have not influenced the development of a liberal democracy in Bosnia, and the best way to help Bosnians would be to delegate the full responsibility of governance to the politicians regardless of the risks. Removal of the OHR, which has long been an integral part of the BiH legal system, could easily paralyze Bosnian politics in the short-run. If the closure takes place without a clear transition strategy for delegating new executive powers to Bosnian state-level institutions, the RS will restrict the functioning of the state. On the other side of the debate are those who argue that there is a real threat to the territorial integrity and sovereignty of BiH from the RS, and the OHR's mission is not over without full implementation of the Dayton Accords. An untimely closure of the OHR would end up in a legal vacuum that might promote instability greater than any other previous political threat to the Dayton Peace Agreement.

CONCLUSION

This chapter evaluated the consociational quality of the Dayton System by looking at four main variables: the formation of grand coalitions between representatives of three constituent nations, the use of the vital national interest veto, the proportionality in political representation, and the level of segmental authority. The misuse of consociational rights to further private interest is endemic in Bosnian politics. The Dayton system has overpowered the entities and blocked cooperation as a viable rational option in the political game. The consociational system forces all players to engage in a game of 'tit-for-tat' on every political issue, only to be resolved through the arbitration of the Office of the High Representative.

The second section evaluated the performance of the Office of High Representative over the past fifteen years, by looking specifically at the use of the nondemocratic Bonn Powers. The international community wants to withdraw from Bosnia by attempting to push Bosnian politicians to work harder for accession to the EU. Nevertheless, the closure of the OHR might cause more harm than good if pursued prematurely without laying out a clear transition plan to domestic state-level authorities. Such a hasty decision would lead to a complete paralysis of the political system in BiH.

The next chapter evaluates the European Union integration process in Bosnian politics by evaluating the political engagement of the EU in BiH.

NOTES

1. Dahl's empirical data supported his reasoning; among 114 polities, 58 percent with a low degree of subcultural pluralism, 36 percent with moderate pluralism, and only 15 percent with marked pluralism were considered polyarchies.

2. Ethnic groups in BiH call themselves *narod*, meaning 'nationalities.'

3. See the discussion on the practice of *Komsiluk* as a form of informal social network.

4. For further details on the form and function of the presidency, please see Article V of the 1995 Dayton Constitution at http://www.ccbh.ba/public/down/US-TAV_BOSNE_I_HERCEGOVINE_engl.pdf.

5. Ibid.

6. Ibid.

7. According to Article VI of the Dayton Constitution, the Constitutional Court is composed of 9 members. "Four members shall be selected by the House of Representatives of the Federation, and two members by the Assembly of the Republika Srpska. The remaining three members shall be selected by the President of the European Court of Human Rights after consultation with the Presidency" with a majority of all members of the Court required to constitute a quorum.

8. Article 4 of the Agreement of the Implementation of the Constituent People's Decision of the Constitutional Court of Bosnia-Herzegovina can be reached at http://www.ohr.int/ohr-dept/legal/const/default.asp?content_id=7274.

9. The complete text of the Venice Commission Report can be reached at http://www.venice.coe.int/docs/2005/CDL-AD(2005)004–e.asp.

10. The applicants, Mr. Sejdić and Mr. Finci, are both prominent public figures. Mr. Sejdić is the Roma Rights Coordinator for the OSCE Mission to Bosnia-Herzegovina, having previously served as Coordinator of the Bosnia-Herzegovina Council for Roma (the highest representative body of the Roma Community in the state) and as a member of the Bosnia-Herzegovina Council of Ministers' Roma Council. Mr. Finci is now serving as Ambassador of Bosnia-Herzegovina to Switzerland, having previously held positions that included being Chair of the Constitutional Commission and the Head of the Civil Service Agency.

11. The ruling of the European Court of Human Rights on the case of Sejdic and Finci vs. Bosnia and Herzegovina on 22 December 2009 is available at http://cmiskp.echr.coe.int/tkp197/view.asp?action=html&documentId=860268&portal=hbkm&source=externalbydocnumber&table=F69A27FD8FB86142BF01C1166DEA398649.

12. Article III of the Dayton Constitution.

13. Information is available at the Republika Srpska Investment Development Bank Report April 2011. Available at http://www.fic.ba/pdf/10–5–2011_monitor07_en.pdf.

14. "The position of High Representative was created under the General Framework Agreement for Peace in BiH (Dayton Peace Agreement) of December 14, 1995 to oversee implementation of the civilian aspects of the Peace Agreement. The mission of the High Representative (who is also the European Union's Special Representative) is to work with the people of BiH and the International Community to ensure that Bosnia-Herzegovina is a peaceful, viable state on course to European integration."

15. Former high representatives of the international community in BiH have been: Carl Bildt (December 1995–June 1997), Carlos Westendorp (June 1997–July 1999), Wolfgang Petritsch (August 1999–May 2002), Paddy Ashdown (June 2002–January 2006), Christian Schwartz-Schilling (February 2006–June 2007), and Miroslav Lajcak (July 2007–March 2009). Valentin Inzko is the current High Representative.

16. Annexes 1A and 1B of the DPA include Military Aspects of the Peace Settlement and Regional Stabilization. Annex 2 covers Inter-Entity Boundary Line and Related Issues whereas Annexes 3, 4, and 5 deal with Elections, Constitution, and Arbitration, respectively. Annex 6 deals with the Human Rights violations, and Annex 7 covers possible problems with the rehabilitation and return of the Refugees and Displaced Persons. Annex 8 sets up a Commission to Preserve National Monuments, and Annex 9 aims to establish joint Bosnia-Herzegovina Public Corporations. Annex 10 establishes the guidelines for the Civilian Implementation of the Peace Settlement, whereas Annex 11 introduces an International Police Task Force under a UN Mandate to tackle organized crime and illegal trafficking.

17. According to the Agreement Pursuant to Article XIV of Annex 6 to the General Framework Agreement for Peace in Bosnia-Herzegovina entered into by the Parties on September 22 and 25, 2003, the Human Rights Chamber's mandate expired on December 31, 2003. This Agreement established the Human Rights Commission to operate between January 1, 2004 and December 31, 2004 within the Constitutional Court of Bosnia-Herzegovina. The Human Rights Commission has jurisdiction to consider pending cases received by the Human Rights Chamber on or before December 31, 2003; after January 1, 2004, new cases alleging human rights violations were to be decided by the Constitutional Court (available at http://www.hrc.ba/). All of the members of the Commission are Bosnian citizens.

18. Mission Implementation Plan (MIP) sets out the core tasks remaining for the OHR. Introduced in 2003 to have the OHR focus its efforts on outstanding priorities, the MIP is updated annually to mark the progress made by the authorities in BiH. As the Bosnian state institutions develop, the MIP has fewer core tasks. Currently three core tasks of the MIP are entrenching the rule of law, reforming the economy, and institution building. The MIP enables the OHR to coordinate the activities of other international actors in each specific reform area. With the closing date of the OHR set for June 2007, the MIP would also be eliminated with the rest of the competencies of the OHR, to be replaced by the core issues identified by the feasibility study of the European Commission and those specific issue areas of the SAA.

19.   Paragraph XI.2 of the Conclusions of the Peace Implementation Conference held in Bonn on December 9–10, 1997 is available at http://www.ohr.int/pic/default.asp?content_id=5182#11.

20.   High Representative's Report to the UN Secretary General can be accessed at http://www.ohr.int/other-doc/hr-reports/default.asp?content_id=3678.

21.   Decision of the OHR, March 7, 2001. The text of the decision can be found at http://www.ohr.int/decisions/removalssdec/default.asp?content_id=328.

22.   Decision of the OHR, April 4, 2002. The text of the decision can be found at http://www.ohr.int/decisions/judicialrdec/default.asp?content_id=7349.

23.   Ashdown's predecessors resorted to the Bonn Powers 323 times between December 1997 and June 2002: one in 1997; thirty-one in 1998; ninety in 1999; eighty-six in 2000; and sixty-two in the first half of 2002. The last in-house comprehensive look by the OHR was conducted in July 2004. It would not be difficult to continue the count beyond July 2004, using the OHR website.

24.   This text is extracted from HR Schwartz-Schilling's first public appearance on Bosnian TV on January 31, 2006. For further details, please see http://www.ohr.int/ohr-dept/presso/presssp/default.asp?content_id=36501.

25.   Schwartz-Schilling's speech can be found at http://www.ohr.int/ohr-dept/presso/presssp/default.asp?content_id=36763.

26.   The Steering Board of the Peace Implementation Council at its meeting in Sarajevo on June 23, 2006, has indicated the board agreed to review and confirm in early 2007 the OHR closure, taking into account the overall situation in BiH and the region. Available at http://www.ohr.int/pic/default.asp?content_id=37503.

27.   The Communiqué of the Steering Board on June 23, 2006, also talks about the creation of a reinforced EUSR: "The EU has decided in principle to reinforce its presence in BiH in the context of the closure of the OHR. The Steering Board welcomed this decision and expressed the view that this could include a role for the EU Special Representative in coordinating meetings of the IC and engaging with BiH counterparts on a range of issues, including maintaining peace and stability and facilitating the continued reform process, including constitutional reform."

28.   Ibid.

29.   The constitutional change package included amendments strengthening the state-level Parliament Assembly: the House of Representatives would have eighty-seven members (instead of the current forty-two) and be responsible for legislative activity. The House of Peoples would have twenty-one (instead of the current 15) members appointed from among the members of the House of Representatives and would see its role limited exclusively to deciding on issues of "vital national interests."

30.   Communique of the PIC Steering Board dated 27 February 2007 is available at http://www.ohr.int/pic/default.asp?content_id=39236.

31.   The 31st Report of the High Representative for Implementation of the Peace Agreement on Bosnia-Herzegovina to the Secretary-General of the United Nations dated May 16, 2007, is available at http://www.ohr.int/other-doc/hr-reports/default.asp?content_id=39813.

32.   The text of the decision on May 30, 2008 is available at http://www.ohr.int/decisions/removalssdec/default.asp?content_id=41770.

33.   Available at http://www.vpi.ba/eng/content/documents/The_Myth_about_the_Closure_of_OHR.pdf .

FOUR

EU Membership Perspective
for Bosnia-Herzegovina

Bosnia-Herzegovina (BiH) has not yet developed any alternative political vision to the EU membership perspective. The reforms embedded in the EU integration process remain the only major challenge to the Dayton System. This chapter is divided into two main sections. The first section presents a chronological overview of the intensifying relations between the EU and BiH. The second section focuses on the goals of the Stabilization and Association Process (SAP) and its evolution through time as the most powerful tool of the EU to push Bosnian politicians toward genuine reforms.

CHRONOLOGY OF EU–BIH RELATIONS

Following the end of the Cold War, the European Union (EU) emerged as an important actor in international politics. Under the protection of NATO's security umbrella, the EU was able to achieve its political goals through nonviolent means of co-option and attraction such as diplomacy, strategic communications, foreign assistance, civic engagement, and economic reconstruction and development. The EU is a soft power that exerts influence without resorting to the use of coercion (Kagan 2002; Nye 2004). Today, the European Union is the largest single unified economic bloc in the world, and the Eurozone countries constitute the second largest economic zone after the United States.

During the 1990s, Central and Eastern European countries undertook fundamental economic and political reforms and adopted the EU Acquis to integrate into the European economic zone that projected constant and robust economic growth. By 2004, the former members of the authoritarian Warsaw bloc had become liberal market economies with functioning parliamentarian regimes. According to pro-European Union scholars, the fast-paced transition of Central and Eastern European countries confirmed the European Union's normative power (Diez 2005; Manners 2006). According to pro-EU scholars, the commitment of the European Union to liberal democratic values, along with its robust economic indicators at the time, influenced democratic transitions in candidate countries.

The Bosnian War Period (1992–1995): Support to Ethnic Division and Embargo

As the crisis in Yugoslavia began to unfold in 1991, the European Community declared itself *primus inter pares* to provide a feasible solution to the crisis. Jacques Poos, the Foreign Minister of Luxembourg who held the rotating EC presidency at the time, declared that it was "the hour of Europe, not the hour of the United States" to solve political matters in the European continent. The European Union (then the European Community, EC), set up a Peace Conference for the Former Yugoslavia. By July 1991, negotiators of the EU Troika[1] convinced the parties to adopt the Brioni Agreement to put an end to the war in Slovenia. The Troika negotiators implemented a number of diplomatic and economic sanctions to force the parties to a negotiated ceasefire agreement by which Yugoslav troops agreed to stop all hostile action on Slovenian territory, while Slovenia and Croatia froze independence activities for a period of three months.[2] However, sharp disagreements existed among the EC member states regarding the recognition of Slovenia and Croatia. Germany announced its intention to recognize these countries in case they decided to declare independence at the end of the three-month freeze period.

The 1991 general elections in BiH by then had already resulted in the formation of a shaky coalition government between the Bosniak, Serbian, and Croatian nationalist parties. When Slovenia and Croatia had finally seceded from Yugoslavia upon Milosevic's insistence on forming a centralized Yugoslavia, BiH found itself in a politically tight spot where a decision had to be made whether and on what grounds Bosnia should seek independence. As was discussed in the previous chapter, the referendum for independence passed with the votes of the Bosniaks and Croats when the Bosnian Serbs decided to boycott.

To prevent further deterioration of the political crisis into a bloody civil war, the EU Peace Conference chair, Lord Carrington, came up with a power-sharing proposal among the Bosniak, Serb, and Croat political powerhouses. The "Carrington-Cutileiro peace plan," which Carrington jointly developed with the Portuguese Ambassador Jorge Cutileiro, proposed ethnic power-sharing on the weak central government level and suggested the devolution of most of the executive and administrative powers from the central government to districts. These districts were to be categorized as Bosniak, Serb, or Croat, even in places where none of the ethnic groups was able to form the majority. The proposal contained a series of measures that would guarantee the protection of minority rights in each ethnic district. The plan was refuted by both the nationalist non-nationalist circles. The non-nationalist circles, including secular and human rights' groups, branded the Carrington-Cutileiro peace plan as further infuriating the ethnic polarization in Bosnia. Furthermore, if the plan were to be implemented, it would force minorities into ethnic enclaves dispersed across the country. Nationalist groups turned down the plan on the grounds that it did not provide clear lines of separation between the proposed ethnic districts. Neither Bosniaks nor Serbs nor Croats would be allowed to run the neighboring districts, so all three were denied the option of partition.

Following the collapse of the plan, in April 1992 Bosnia-Herzegovina went ahead with the independence declaration despite the protests of the Bosnian Serbs. The EU recognized the independence immediately. The Bosnian Serb paramilitary forces with the covert assistance from the Yugoslav National Army began pushing for territorial advances from Northwestern Bosnia toward the Serbian border on the east. Croatian nationalist paramilitaries entered the war in mid-1992. By the end of 1992, the country was caught in full-fledged civil war.

With the intensification of the conflict in BiH in the second half of 1992, the United Nations intervened. Efforts of the European Community became a part of UN attempts to bring an end to the conflict through peaceful means. Prominent members of the EC such as France, UK, and Germany took part in the diplomatic efforts, implementation of sanctions, and the provision of humanitarian aid. A good example of renewed EC efforts is the International Conference on the Former Yugoslavia

CROATIA   Osijek   VOJVODINA

Novi Sad

Banja Luka   Brcko

Bihac

BOSNIA   Tuzla

Knin   Srebrenica
Zepa

Livno
Split   Sarajevo
Gorazde

Mostar

Carrington-Cutileiro
Peace Plan
[ ] Muslim cantons
[ ] Serbian cantons
[ ] Croatian cantons

MONTENEGRO

Podgorica
Dubrovnik

Figure 4.1.   Carrington-Cutileiro Peace Plan distribution of ethnic districts

launched in Geneva, under the auspices of the UN represented by American Cyrus Vance and Britain's Lord Owen acting on behalf of the EC. In early January 1993, Vance and Lord Owen began negotiating a peace proposal with the leaders of Bosnia's warring factions. The Vance-Owen Plan was the last proposal that tried to maintain a multiethnic, centralized Bosnia-Herzegovina, which either reinforced or recognized elements of partition. The plan proposed the division of BiH into ten semi-autonomous regions and was politically backed by the UN. On May 5, however, the self-proclaimed Bosnian Serb Assembly refused the Vance-Owen plan; and on June 18, Lord Owen declared that the plan was "dead." The plan failed due to the rapid pace of territorial division, fragmentation, and ethnic cleansing taking place during the negotiations for the proposal. The plan was already irrelevant by the time it was announced.[3] Likewise, a new regime of sanctions was approved by subsequent UNSC Resolutions[4] with the commitment of EC/EU assistance in enforcing the sanctions that banned trade between Bosnia's neighbors and BiH and introduced an arms embargo. The European Community became an important component in the provision of humanitarian aid. Meanwhile, the member states supplied troops for the United Nations Protection Force (UNPROFOR) mission.[5]

In the face of a brutal partition war, the EU negotiators, with US and Russian cooperation, tried a third version of the ethnic power-sharing formula. In May 1993, the United States, Russia, Britain, France, and Spain developed a Joint Action Plan for a union of three republics. The plan sealed off Bosnian borders, and extended the UNPROFOR's mandate to include the protection of Bosnia's three eastern enclaves and the towns of Sarajevo, Bihac, and Tuzla. The Joint Action Plan was widely seen as a harbinger of the next stage of talks, toward a three-way partition. Assuming tacit acceptance of their war aims, Serbian nationalists responded quickly with a map for the Serbian republic, which would

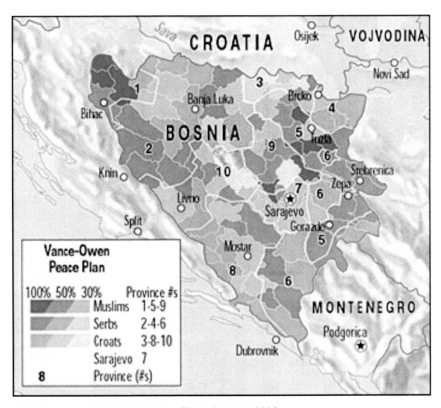

Figure 4.2.   Vance-Owen Peace Plan, January 1993

comprise over 60 percent of Bosnia. While Serbian and Croatian paramilitaries continued their offensives on Bosniak held territory, EU negotiators were bargaining over the territory to be allocated to the three proposed republics. By late September, they came to an agreement on the boundaries of the three republics, and agreed that Sarajevo and Mostar would be placed under UN and EU administrations respectively. The Serbian republic would constitute 53 percent of Bosnia-Herzegovina, the Croatian republic 17 percent, and the Bosniak republic 30 percent. The allocation was not demographically proportionate—Serbs comprised some 37 percent of the population of Bosnia while Bosniaks made up 43 percent—but was supposed to conform to prewar landholdings (the predominantly peasant Serbs farmed some 51 percent of Bosnia).

Serbian and Croatian nationalists saw the Union of Three Republics Plan as similar to a three-way partition, and their respective nationalist leaders, Radovan Karadzic and Mate Boban, confidently styled them-

Figure 4.3.   The Union of Three Republics Plan, September 1993

selves the presidents of Herceg-Bosna and Republika Srpska. As with the previous peace plans, Bosnia's Muslims (Bosniaks) were the chief sufferers. The Bosniak republic would be fragmented, with Bihac isolated in the northwest and the eastern enclaves connected only by a road. It would also be landlocked and dependent on the Serbian and Croatian republics for access to the sea, as well as access to its one-time neighbors, Serbia and Croatia. The Bosniak republic's viability was questionable. More importantly, so was its identity. Thus far, the leading Bosniak political party that led the Bosnian government had striven for secularism, especially the separation of the church from state (in sharp contrast to the leading Serbian and Croatian political parties). It was doubtful whether Bosniak secularism would continue after partition. The Bosnian parliament turned down the proposal, and the war dragged on.

In 1994, as the humanitarian catastrophe grew worse in Bosnia-Herzegovina, a Contact Group of influential powers was formed with the aim of bringing coherence to the international community's policies on the Bosnian War. The Contact Group initially had six members: the US, the UK, Russia, Italy, Germany, and France. The European Union was entirely excluded from the negotiation table. Although using the Contact Group as a platform to make the EU visible along with other international powers could have been a possibility, the form and function of the Group remained as an initiative of and for its five constituent members.[6] The endgame in Bosnia came only after images from the genocide at Srebrenica and massacres at the City Central Market in Sarajevo hit TV screens all around the world. The general public was outraged by the passivity of the international community to the point where the UNSC had to call in NATO forces for immediate action to put an end to the conflict (Woodward 1995). The US and the Contact Group spearheaded the international efforts during the endgame of the conflict, as support for NATO's military intervention in BiH was growing.[7] Following the heavy bombardment of Bosnian Serb positions by NATO forces, and the advances of the Bosniak-Croat army toward Banja Luka, negotiations for a peace settlement took place in Dayton, Ohio. The role of Carl Bildt as the EU's Representative at the negotiation table was to outline the future civilian involvement of the EU in the immediate postconflict phase rather than to design a political role for the EU.

The inability of the EU to stop the war in BiH demonstrated that the EC/EU was a political light-weight with unclear, contradictory policies among its members. The lack of a common European identity in foreign policy and on security and defense issues cost the European Union a loss of face and political influence in the immediate postconflict phase. In the short term, the EU had to leverage its stronger economic power to alter the postconflict developments in Bosnia.

Postconflict Reconstruction in BiH (1996–1999): The EU in Search of a Strategy

As part of the international community's concerted efforts in the immediate postconflict period, the European Union undertook the reconstruction and development of the economic infrastructure, while overseeing the liberalization of the state economy. At the Madrid European Council (December 15–16, 1995), following the signing of the Dayton Peace Agreement in Paris, the EU expressed its commitment to the task of reconstruction by reaffirming:

> Its willingness to contribute to the international effort aimed at reconstruction of the regions devastated by the war once peace is established. To that end the EU will co-ordinate its actions with other members of the international community in order to provide long-term assistance with the objectives of supporting economic development, reinforcement of civil society and reconciliation and regional economic cooperation. In the perspective of peace, the EU is developing its long-term policy toward the region, to help build stability and prosperity.[8]

In the immediate postconflict period, BiH benefited from the humanitarian assistance programs of the ECHO (European Commission Humanitarian Aid Office), and, from 1996 onward, from trade preferences. BiH was also allowed to use funds from the PHARE (Poland and Hungary: Assistance for Restructuring their Economies) and OBNOVA (focused regional assistance on postconflict reconstruction, return of refugees, regional cooperation and reconciliation) programs until they were all pooled into the CARDS (Community Assistance for Reconstruction, Development and Stabilization) program in 2001.[9]

In February 1996, the EU decided to adopt a regional approach to the Western Balkans to encourage partnerships between the neighboring countries of the region as a way to consolidate peace in the region:

> Application of the agreements will be subject, particularly where economic cooperation is concerned, to the readiness of each of the countries concerned to cooperate with its neighbors. They will have to undertake to adopt reciprocal measures, particularly regarding the free

movement of goods and persons and the provision of services, and to develop projects of common interest. Through this regional approach, financial aid from the European Union were oriented toward jointly defined, and cross-border projects.[10]

Beginning in 1997, leveraging the overwhelming demand for its assistance programs, the EU developed the idea of "conditionality" to push for political and economic reforms. The General Affairs Council (GAC) defines conditionality as follows:

> Political and economic conditions are the basis for a coherent and transparent policy toward the development of bilateral relations in the field of trade, financial assistance and economic cooperation as well as of contractual relations. The EU strategy should serve as an incentive, not as an obstacle to the countries concerned to fulfill these conditions.[11]

Fulfilling the economic and political conditionalities of the EU had become a prerequisite for receiving reconstruction and development assistance from the Community Budget for all of the Western Balkan countries, and for BiH in particular. The idea of conditionality is built on the liberal belief that transitioning into a functioning market economy needs to be accompanied by the liberalization of the human rights regime, consolidation of democratic practices, and rule of law. With the use of the conditionality principle as a tool, the EU aimed to promote closer cooperation in the Western Balkans, envisioning a structural solution to conflicts in the long run. Nevertheless during this period the EU did not have the means and the drive to make any political commitment on the future status of the Western Balkans. In December 1998, the European Union Council decided to adopt a common strategy toward the Western Balkans, but such strategy did not include any perspective for the future integration of the region into the EU.[12] The European Commission's top priority was the economic facilitation of the Central and Eastern Europe Countries' integration into the Union (Friis and Murphy 2000). The political future of the Western Balkans came much later in the list of things to do.

EU Membership Perspective and Stabilization and Association Process (SAP) in BiH (1999–Present)

The EU's involvement in BiH changed dramatically during this period. Its prior agenda of providing development and reconstruction assis-

tance transformed to one focused on the promotion of the EU membership as the only viable future for a united BiH. On May 26, 1999, the
European Commission proposed the initiation of the new Stabilization
and Association Process for five countries of the Western Balkans, including BiH. The main objectives of the process were outlined as: "drawing
the region closer to the prospect of full integration into EU structures,
and supporting the consolidation of democracy, rule of law, economic
development and reform, adequate administrative structures, and regional cooperation."[13]

The Stabilization and Association Process (SAP) has become the most
important policy tool of the EU through which Bosnia's progress is evaluated. The SAP is an integral part of the enlargement process; it sets the
framework of the relationship with the EU for the Western Balkan countries, all the way to their future accession. The Stabilization and Association Process aims to put Bosnia-Herzegovina on the European integration
track while employing the conditionality principle to promote reforms on
different sectors of socioeconomic and political life. The SAP is supposed
to serve as a policy tool that would encourage nonethnic politics,
strengthen the rule of law, generate a functioning market economy, and
combat corruption and organized crime. The EU intended the development of strong links between BiH and the EU through the three main
mechanisms of trade, financial assistance, and contractual relations. The
EU involvement in that period (1996–2003) consisted of billions of Euros
worth of financial assistance for postconflict reconstruction and relief efforts, which made the EU the largest donor in BiH from the international
community.[14]

The possibility of future membership of the Western Balkan countries
in the EU was first mentioned in the European Council's Feira Summit in
June 2000, with the statement that all the Stabilization and Association
countries are "potential candidates " for EU membership:

> The European Council confirms that its objective remains the fullest
> possible integration of the countries of the region into the political and
> economic mainstream of Europe through the Stabilization and Associa-
> tion Process, political dialogue, liberalization of trade and cooperation
> in Justice and Home Affairs. All the countries concerned are potential
> candidates for EU membership. The Union will support the Stabiliza-
> tion and Association Process through technical and economic assis-
> tance. The Commission presented proposals to the Council to stream-
> line and accelerate the procedures for disbursement of assistance and

the early extension of asymmetrical industrial and agricultural trade benefits to the Balkan States.[15]

On November 24, 2000, the Zagreb Summit officially endorsed the SAP by the EU and the Western Balkan countries (including BiH). In return for the offer of accession on the basis of the Treaty on European Union (TEU), the 1993 Copenhagen criteria, and an assistance program to support that ambition, the Western Balkan countries were to abide by the EU's conditionality principle and use the Stabilization and Association Process, and in particular the Stabilization and Association Agreements when signed, as the means to begin to prepare themselves for the demands of perspective on accession to the EU:

> The European Union confirms its wish to contribute to the consolidation of democracy and to give its resolute support to the process of reconciliation and cooperation between the countries concerned. It reaffirms the European perspective of the countries participating in the stabilization and association process and their status as potential candidates for membership in accordance with the Feira conclusions.[16]

Between 2001 and 2006, the CARDS (Community Assistance for Reconstruction, Development and Stabilization) program became the main community support mechanism of the EU, specifically designed for the Stabilization and Association countries. The CARDS program served the overall EU political objectives in the Western Balkans and BiH and operates through conditionality as well:

> The existing community assistance should be expanded and redirected to adjust it to the European Union's political objectives for the region and, particularly, to contribute to the stabilization and association process and increase the responsibility of recipient countries and entities in relation to that process. . . . A precondition for receiving assistance is that the recipients respect democratic principles, the rule of law, human and minority rights, fundamental freedoms and the principles of international law (Articles 5 and 7 of the European Council Regulation (EC) No 2666/2000).[17]

At the Thessaloniki Summit in June 2003, the SAP was confirmed as the EU policy for the Western Balkans. The EU perspective for these countries was confirmed. The Thessaloniki Summit is a contract between the EU and the Western Balkan countries where the EU acknowledged that:

> the Stabilization and Association Process (SAP) will remain the framework for the European course of the Western Balkan countries, all the

way to their future accession. The process and the prospects it offers serve as the anchor for reform in the Western Balkans, in the same way the accession process has done in Central and Eastern Europe. Progress of each country toward the EU will depend on its own merits in meeting the Copenhagen criteria and the conditions set for the SAP and confirmed in the final declaration of the November 2000 Zagreb summit.

The representatives of the Western Balkan countries at the summit responded to the acknowledgement of the EU by welcoming:

> The decisions by the EU to strengthen its Stabilization and Association policy toward the region and to enrich it with elements from the experience of enlargement. They welcome in particular the launching of the European Partnerships, as well as the decisions for enhanced cooperation in the areas of political dialogue and the Common Foreign and Security Policy, parliamentary co-operation, support for institution building, opening of Community programmes. They take note of the ongoing discussions for an increase in the budgeted Community financial support to the region through the CARDS programme. [18]

Following the Thessaloniki Summit, the relationship between the EU and BiH became more institutionalized through programs in which conditionality formed the core. Between 2001 and 2006, BiH made use of €412 million of CARDS Program Funds, whereas the total EU financial assistance added up to €1.952 billion in the postconflict period in BiH. [19] With the signing of the SAA in June 2008, BiH and the EU entered an official contractual relationship where BiH has to complete reforms on market liberalization and institution building to qualify for candidate status. The European Union allocated a total of €488 million between 2008 and 2013 under the Instrument for Pre-Accession Assistance (IPA) Program for BiH to be used in transition assistance and institution building and cross-border cooperation. [20] Unfortunately, the lack of political stability in BiH has put the use of the funds at risk. Below is a concise history of the road BiH had to travel since the inception of the SAP tool.

The road to EU integration is said to be the result of a partnership, through which priorities are identified together, while only one of the *partners* is eligible to evaluate whether the priorities have been met with the necessary reforms. The reframing of the conditionality principle as a partnership has proven to be disappointing even for those directly involved in the integration process. The issue of easing visa requirements has been on the agenda of EU–BiH relations since the Thessaloniki Summit in June 2003. Only in 2007 did the European Council agree to ease the visa requirements for the country in 2008 and the visa regime was finally abolished in December 2010.

Roadmap for BiH (March 2000–September 2002)

The roadmap for BiH was established in March 2000, as the starting point of BiH's long road to EU membership. The roadmap included reforms in four areas: economy, democracy, human rights, and rule of law.[21] It identified eighteen priority reform steps, quick wins that aimed at strengthening of governance structures at the state level, paving the way for future reforms as Bosnia progresses, and generating a working human rights regime with the adoption of necessary legal procedures. Until September 2002, the EU/BiH Consultative Task Force (CTF)[22] had eleven meetings to facilitate the reform process. The roadmap reforms underlined the need for a liberal integrated market economy and politically capable state-level institutions to benefit from the EU integration.

The economic liberalization steps included the abolishment of the socialist era Payment Bureau, the establishment of a State Treasury, and the removal of all trade barriers between the Federation and RS markets. The political institutionalization reforms set benchmarks for establishing a functioning electoral system, combating corruption, establishing a Civil Service Law, and encouraging refugee returns to their preconflict properties in both entities. In the fields of democracy, human rights, and rule of law, some of the steps to be followed warranted a stronger engagement at all levels to create the conditions for sustainable returns and implementation of the decisions of the European Court of Human Rights.

After eleven meetings of the EU/Bosnia-Herzegovina Consultative Task Force (CTF), the European Commission declared that the roadmap was "substantially completed" on September 19, 2002.[23] This announcement aimed to boost the reputation of the non-nationalist parties before the general elections on October 5. The European Commissioner for External Relations Chris Patten's comments on that day clearly summarized the EU's policy of leveraging the accession process as a tool to transform Bosnia's democracy:

> BiH has made progress toward democracy, peace, economic reform and self-sustainability. However, much remains to be done and BiH must continue to intensify reform. The prospect of a feasibility report is a reason to step up efforts, not an excuse to relax. The European Union

is committed to assist Bosnia-Herzegovina with reform. However, we expect a matching commitment from the new government at all levels. I hope too, that the people of Bosnia-Herzegovina will turn out to vote on October 5, and that they will use their democratic rights to choose a modern European future for BiH.

Feasibility Study Reforms (November 2003–November 2005)

The design of the feasibility study was a joint effort by the Directorate for European Integration (DEI) and the European Commission. DEI is established as a response to the demand of the EU member states to have a counterpart at the BiH state level that would conduct policy and strategy formulation for EU integration, assist in the negotiation and implementation of the SAA (Stabilization and Association Agreement), and lead the programming and implementation of EC assistance.[24]

In March 2003, a questionnaire was given to the DEI covering all sectors relevant to a future Stabilization and Association Agreement (SAA) with the EU. The answers of the DEI were later discussed with the Commission in a series of working groups between May and September 2003. In November 2003, the European Commission produced a feasibility study assessing BiH's capacity to implement a future Stabilization and Association Agreement with the EU. The belief in the merit of the use of conditionality is evident in the text of the study. The study concluded that negotiations for the SAA were to be initiated once BiH's political leadership agreed to make progress on sixteen key priorities. These priorities aim to enhance the competencies of the state institutions, as well as the quality of the services provided by the government institutions. In the document, the EU urged compliance with existing conditionality and international obligations, more effective governance, more effective public administration, European integration, effective human rights provisions, an effective judiciary, tackling organized crime, managing asylum and migration, customs and taxation reform, budget legislation, budget practice, reliable statistics, consistent trade policy, an integrated energy market, a BiH single economic space, and public broadcasting.[25]

The findings of the feasibility study constitute the basis of the relationship between the EU and BiH. The extent of progress on some of the priorities identified in the feasibility study was to determine the progress of Bosnia toward the signing of the Stabilization and Association Agreement.

Negotiations for the SAA (June 2004–June 2008)

The EU–Western Balkans Summit in Thessaloniki on the 19th and 20th of June 2003 started a new phase in the EU's involvement in Bosnia under the heading of European Partnership to materialize the European perspective. The Thessaloniki Summit strengthened the Stabilization and Association Process with elements inspired by the preaccession process that led to ten new member states joining the Union in May 2004. On June 14, 2004, the European Union Council initiated the European Partnership with Bosnia-Herzegovina.[26] European Partnerships set definite principles and priorities for the host Western Balkan country to accomplish by taking initiative. In order to prepare for further integration with the European Union, Bosnia-Herzegovina was expected to develop a plan with a timetable and measures to address the priorities of this European Partnership. It was thought that clear-cut key, short-term, and mid-term priorities would bring momentum to the integration process. The European Partnership recognizes that the main task of the EU integration in Bosnia-Herzegovina is to bring political stability to the country via its association and harmonization with the EU legislation. The European Partnership sets the structure of the EU–BiH relations in an asymmetric fashion, which sets the European Union as the partner making decisions on the principles, priorities, and conditions, as well as any ensuing adjustments.[27] As the executive body of the EU, the European Council is given the mandate to renew priorities for further work, on the basis of the findings of the European Commission's Progress Reports on Bosnia-Herzegovina. The European Commission evaluates Bosnia's progress on a regular basis through annual progress reports upon new priorities and conditions are introduced.

In November 2005, the EU Commission judged that BiH had made sufficient progress in the implementation of the feasibility study reforms and recommended the initiation of negotiations to sign the SAA with BiH. SAA negotiations between the EU and BiH were officially launched more than a year after the inception of the European Partnership.

The European Partnership is a part of the Stabilization and Association Process, as stated in its principles: "The Stabilization and Association Process (SAP) remains the framework for the European course of the Western Balkan countries, all the way to their future accession."[28]

The EU intends to leverage the accession process as a permanent conflict transformation tool. The main priorities identified for Bosnia-Herzegovina relate primarily to its capacity to meet:

- the Copenhagen criteria defined in 1993;
- the conditions set for the Stabilization and Association Process (Council conclusions of April 29, 1997 and June 21 and 22, 1999);
- the 2000 Zagreb declaration; and
- the Thessaloniki Agenda of 2003.

European Partnership as a Tool for Democratization

The short- and medium-term priorities are classified as follows:

- The key priorities: the reform of the police forces; full cooperation with the International Criminal Tribunal for the former Yugoslavia (ICTY); reform of public broadcasting; implementation of the public-administration reform strategy adopted in 2006; reinforcement of administrative capacities in order to implement the Stabilization and Association Agreement (SAA); settlement of bilateral issues; creation of an internal single economic space; correction of structural rigidities impeding the functioning of the labor market; improvement of the functioning and viability of institutional structures; and respect of human rights and fundamental freedoms, including, if necessary, reform of the constitutional framework;
- The political criteria: democracy and the rule of law (constitution, governance, electoral legislation, public administration and service, the judicial system and anticorruption policy), human rights and the protection of minorities (repeal of the death penalty in the constitution of the Republika Srpska; compliance with international standards and conventions, including those of the Council of Europe; access to justice; reform of the prison system; social inclusion; and the rights and protection of minorities, including the Roma), regional issues, and international obligations;
- The economic criteria: macroeconomic and financial stability, the acceleration and completion of privatizations, budgetary supervision mechanisms, the quality of public finances, the reconciliation of domestic claims, greater legal certainty for economic operators, better corporate governance, and a better (legal, regulatory, tax,

judicial, etc.) environment for companies and business, and preparations for membership of the World Trade Organization (WTO);

• European standards relating to the Community acquis as regards the internal market, EU sectoral policies, and the area of justice, freedom, and security. Bosnia-Herzegovina must endeavor to bring its legislation into line with the Community acquis in these areas and ensure its implementation.

The Commission's assessments of developments in Bosnia-Herzegovina are based in particular on the priorities identified by the Partnership.

Key priorities focus on reform in police structures, public broadcasting system, public administration, integration of the internal market and strengthening of the state-level institutions. These reform demands underline the indirect involvement of the EU in state-building. The midterm priorities of the European Partnership are mostly political ones, reminding the BiH political authorities to take the necessary measures to fulfill their obligations in line with membership requirements of the international organizations, such as the Council of Europe. They focus on the consolidation of the democratic qualities of the regime and strengthen the rule of law throughout the country. In that respect, the state-building measures of the key term priorities are further supported by the midterm goals of democracy-building as BiH progresses to full membership with the help of the European Partnership. The conditionality principle is at the core of the European Partnership:

> Community assistance under the Stabilization and Association Process to the Western Balkan countries is conditional on further progress in satisfying the Copenhagen criteria as well as progress in meeting the specific priorities of this European Partnership.[29]

The EU officials in Sarajevo promote the use of the conditionality principle as an indication of the EU's unique focus on domestic ownership of the reform process. According to the conditionality principle, Bosnian politicians are rewarded for progress instead of being penalized in cases of stagnation and setbacks. Yet the European Union falls into the same trap as the international community. While arguing for the necessity of ownership of the reform process by the Bosnians, the EU threatens BiH politicians with cutting community assistance to the country (mainly the CARDS/IPA program) should they decide not to implement the reforms as outlined in the European Partnership document. This is a coercive and punitive document, imposing democratization à la Europe.

Failure of the European Partnership

Once the short- and mid-term priorities indicated in the Partnership document are concluded, it would mean that Bosnian democracy and state structures have reached European Union standards. The problem with this approach is the assumption that the EU guidelines and templates are beneficial in the long run. However, this assumption blurs the vision of the policy makers in Brussels in that they seem to forget that imposed ownership of reforms is not genuine, just like imposed democratization does not replace genuine democratization. Using the conditionality principle in a negative manner reproduces the nondemocratic involvement of the international community in the context of EU integration.

The constant stagnation in BiH's integration process points to deficits in the structure and functioning of the European Partnership. The European Partnership fails to generate political will among Bosnian politicians for the reforms. The political leadership of the three constituent nations disagree on the form and extent of the reforms. As a consequence of their disagreement, the European Partnership document, with its key short-term and mid-term priorities, loses its leverage. In the face of the social and ethnic fragmentation of Bosnian politics, the conditionality principle works in reverse and highlights the political cleavages between the parties. Bosnian leaders do not see EU membership as a realistic goal in the medium term that is worth giving up the ethno-nationalist rhetoric that works in their favor during the electoral season.[30]

Since 2006, the European Union has allowed BiH move forward in the integration process although most of the key reforms in the European Partnership document have not been fully implemented. As of 2011, the public broadcasting system has not been unified in the Federation due to the veto of vital national interest by the Croat political leadership. Police forces formally remain disintegrated among the two entities. The internal market of BiH is still divided in two; two separate privatization processes take place in Republika Srpska and the Federation as nationalistic competition among the entities.

The Case of Police Reform as a Failure of European Partnership

Police reform emerged as one of the most urgent issues in 2006 and 2007, a period when Bosnia-Herzegovina was striving to sign the Stabilization and Association Agreement. The Guiding Principles on Police Reform (three requirements of the European Commission from Article 1 of the Agreement on Restructuring of Police Structures of October 2005) are as follows:

1. All legislative and budgetary competencies for all matters are *to be vested at the state level*.
2. *No political interference* in the operational work of the police.
3. *Functional local areas* are to be determined by technical policing criteria.[31]

Police reform impacts the everyday life of ordinary citizens. The police, in comparison with the army, are much more connected with the culture, administrative arrangement, tradition, and the laws of the country. A report of the International Crisis Group (ICG) claims that Bosnia-Herzegovina has long needed substantive police reform (2005).[32] During the 1992–1995 war, the police were used as a key instrument of ethnic cleansing—particularly in Republika Srpska (RS) and the Croatian areas of the Federation—to build ethnically homogenous territories. The war left Bosnia with three police forces: Bosniak, Croat, and Serb, each with its own jurisdictions. The first two have since joined, at least technically, but the RS has declined all efforts to reform its structures or integrate them with those of the other ethnic groups.

Among the three principles, two of them are related to the sovereignty concerns of the RS. The crossing of the Inter-Entity Border Line in ten different places was not perceived as a technical matter of creating functional police areas, but as an attempt to destroy the territorial integrity of RS. An article by the relatively liberal media professional Vaskovic[33] in the pro-EU *Patriot* magazine is a reliable indicator of this bitter sentiment as he mentions a crucial detail: "there are now twelve existing police administrations (eleven in the Federation, one in the Republic), under the new plan, there would be ten. This is no doubt an attempt to abolish the Republika Srpska."[34] It is easy to understand how the 'administrative rationalization' argument of the EU principle falls short of convincing a liberal opinion leader in the RS when the focus is not the ten times more complex Federation structure, but the Republika Srpska. The proposed police reform inevitably looked like a centralization push by the European community disguised as curbing bureaucracy.

Another principle proposed by the police reform was the transfer of all legislative and budgetary competencies for all police matters to the state level. The essential part of this reform was the fact that local police forces will be responsible to the state authorities, not to the entity authorities, through the chain of command. According to a report produced by the Police Reform Directorate[35] on how to implement the 'much-needed' reform, local authorities such as the cantons in the federation, both entities, and the Brcko district would have a right to control security but not to manage the police.[36] This was not considered as an acceptable proposal by the RS leadership.

Police reform did not envision any dramatic changes; the police officers in the RS were to be maintained for the foreseeable future, and only the structure and the chain of command would be changed. The implementation plan foresaw transitional periods for the changes to take place, which would last until the proper laws were fully adopted; a timeline of five years was given as the expected time of transition. It looked like the members of the Police Reform Directorate had reached a compromise. Yet maintaining the operational command of the police forces while giving up control over the budget allocations of the RS police, upset the Bosnian Serb political leadership. Dodik, in 2006, clearly stated that Bosnian Serb leadership would not tolerate the loss of their police force and indicated they would agree only to a partial unification that would leave their interior ministry intact.[37]

As a response, the European Commission delegated the use of political muscle to the EU Special Representative Miroslav Lajcak, who at the time was also acting as the High Representative of the international community. Lajcak did not threaten the Bosnian politicians with the use of the Bonn Powers. Instead, he facilitated forming neutral platforms around which politicians from the RS and the Federation could discuss their differences on the implementation of the demanded police reform and try to find common ground. Leveraging his role as the EU Special Representative, Lajcak adapted the role of an honest broker promising the Bosnian politicians that he could convince the European Commission to move forward with the SAA once a show of goodwill was made by the politicians. Another tactic he used during this process was to underline the approaching deadline for an agreement. He associated himself with the EU integration prospect of BiH clearly in his press declarations and public appearances. He began to promote the signing of the SAA as the only panacea against nationalist politics. Lajcak warned the Bosnian politicians that it was their last chance if they were sincere about EU membership. At the end, a last minute deal was secured among the Bosnian politicians known as the "Mostar Declaration on honoring the commitments for implementation of the police reform with an aim to initial and sign the Stabilization and Association Agreement" in October 2007. The Declaration was deemed sufficient by the EU to give the green light to go ahead with the signing of the Stabilization and Association Agreement in June 2008. The Stabilization and Association Agreement was signed in June 2008.

Below is the text of the Mostar Declaration:

DECLARATION

The signatories of the present Declaration agree to undertake all necessary activities for implementation of the police reform in accordance with the principles of the European Union, and which are indispensable for continuing the process of association of Bosnia-Herzegovina with the European Union.

We fully and unconditionally agree with the content of the present Declaration and every of its particular point as indicated below.

I. The reform of the current police structures in Bosnia-Herzegovina shall be implemented in line with the following three principles of the European Commission:

1. All legislative and budgetary competencies for all police matters must be vested at the State level
2. No political interference with operational policing
3. Functional local police areas must be determined by technical policing criteria, where operational command is exercised at the local level.

II. Accordingly, we agree and accept that:

- the overall reform aims at establishing a functional, multiethnic and professional police on the basis of the three principles of the European Commission, and which shall guarantee the security of all citizens and goods on the entire territory of BiH
- the structure of the single police forces of Bosnia-Herzegovina shall be in line with the constitutional structure of the country

- new and reformed police structure of Bosnia-Herzegovina shall be based on relevant provisions of the Constitution of BiH, which shall take form during the process of constitutional reform.
- the details of the police structure of BiH shall be defined through two fundamental laws: Law on police service of BiH and Law on Police officials of BiH.

Being aware of the gravity of political momentum in Bosnia-Herzegovina, and of the need to continue as soon as possible on the road of European integrations, the signatories of the present Declaration commit themselves to proceed, without delay, to a full implementation of the above mentioned principles.

The European Union circles in Sarajevo and Brussels knew beforehand that there was a slim chance of the Bosnian politicians implementing the decisions of the Mostar Declaration. Nevertheless, the EU wanted to demonstrate that it was in charge of the tense political situation in Bosnia-Herzegovina. The Mostar Declaration provided that opportunity. The European Union hailed the agreement as a turning point for BiH, and the SAA was signed in June 2008. The implementation of the reform became, rather, a nuisance to be dealt with in the indefinite future. What mattered at the moment was taking BiH into the SAA wagon. So far, none of the articles agreed on in the Declaration has been implemented; the fate of police reform in Bosnia-Herzegovina remains unclear.

Below is an analysis of the general image of the EU in Bosnia-Herzegovina. The responses provided by the field interviewees support the arguments above. Unclear, contradictory policies by the EU carry the risk of making the EU a weak political actor in BiH.

PERCEPTIONS OF STRENGTHS AND WEAKNESSES OF THE EU INTEGRATION POLICY IN BIH

The results summarized in table 4.1 are derived from interviews conducted with EU officials in three different time intervals between 2005 and 2010 in Sarajevo and Brussels. A majority of the responses indicate that EU officials regard EU policies in BiH as noninterventionist, but still strong enough to generate political clout through the use of conditionalities of the European Partnership without violating the sovereignty of Bosnia-Herzegovina. According to the EU officials, EU policies do not

Table 4.1.   Strengths of the EU policies in Bosnia-Herzegovina according to EU officials

Responses by the EU officials	#
Not interventionist	7
No imposition of value transition	7
Political leverage and assistance without touching the sovereignty	7
Transforms the Bosnian society	4
Vehicle for socio-economic development	4
Clear commitment to BiH's future in the EU	3
Unity of purpose among all EU organs	3
Facilitates technical adaptation	1
Does not dictate reforms	1
Promotes inter-ethnic collaboration	1
Replaces imposition of the International Community	1
Is developed with local counterparts	1
Total	40

impose any value change on Bosnian politicians, yet somehow manage to transform Bosnian society through the facilitation of adaptation of laws and regulations. There is a sense of institutional self-righteousness in the responses, such as the belief that the EU reforms promote interethnic collaboration, and that the reform priorities are developed jointly with local counterparts. There is a certain amount of embedded jingoism in the responses, such as the argument that the pull of the EU integration process will replace the push of the international community.

The findings in table 4.2 display a list of perceptions about the weaknesses of the EU policy in BiH as perceived by Bosnian politicians and the representatives of the international community interviewed in three different intervals between 2005 and 2010. Contrary to the perceptions of strengths identified by the EU officials in table 4.2, a significant portion of Bosnian politicians and representatives of the international community interviewed see the noninterventionist character of the EU policies in BiH as a lack of political muscle, a major weakness. Formulaic politics are considered a sign of weakness by many Bosnian politicians and within the international community. In an accession process, as a rule, the European Commission develops a formula, or a set of steps, like it did in BiH

Table 4.2. Weaknesses of the EU policy in BiH according to Bosnian politicians and representatives of the international community

Responses	#
Has no political muscle	25
Unclear	25
Imploring	25
Contradictory	25
Insists on formal politics	11
Unfocused	12
Not enough promotion of the EU integration	5
Ignores the youth	2
Tolerates radical politicians	2
Ignores human rights violations	1
Total	133

with the roadmap, feasibility study and stabilization and association process, which Bosnian politicians are expected to perform. The Commission evaluates the progress of the country in its annual progress reports and makes suggestions to the European Council, which makes the political decision. Ideally, in such a structured process, the applicant country is not expected to have many problems with the conclusion of the necessary reforms. Nevertheless, in Bosnia, each reform agenda causes another heated political debate between the nationalist politicians of the constituent nations, resulting in underperformance and failure, contrary to the self-perceptions of the EU officials. Instead of admitting the failure of the formulaic policies, the EU accepts the unsubstantiated promises of Bosnian politicians as sufficient to prove its self-righteousness, at the cost of disintegrating the country further.

Another significant weakness emphasized is that the EU policies remain unfocused and fail to provide clear and strong responses against the daily provocations of radical Bosnian politicians, violations of human rights, and the high level of unemployment among youth. A significant chunk of this critique came from Bosnian politicians who claimed that the EU constantly changed positions on key issues through time, as was the case in the failed police reform. It remained unclear until the signing of the SAA whether the implementation of the reform or the agreement on the need to carry out the reform was the necessary condition. Until very recently, the political representation of the EU in BiH was provided through three different channels: the European Union Special Representative, the Embassy of the EU member state holding the rotating EU presidency, and the Head of the European Commission Delegation.[38] More often than not, these three posts delivered contradictory messages regarding the progress of the reform process and on the further steps to be taken. The lack of progress in areas like the police reform, the constitutional reform process, public broadcasting reform, and the re-allocation of state property characterizes EU policies in BiH as imploring and lacking in substance. In table 4.1, one of the strengths of EU policies identified by EU officials was the transformative power of the technical adaptation process. Bosnian politicians and the representatives of the international community interviewed, on the other hand, see this as a significant impediment that limits the effectiveness of the EU policies in Bosnia. This is why the Mostar declaration remained only as a declaration, and the police reform was never implemented.

CONCLUSION

After the signing of the Stabilization and Association Agreement (SAA) in June 2008, the most substantial development in BiH has been the signing of the visa liberalization agreement. Visa liberalization has been one area of reform where all Bosnians, regardless of their ethnic groups, wanted to benefit from. In June 2008, the EU provided a roadmap for visa liberalization. BiH was asked to upgrade the management of its state borders and integrate them under the unified State Border Service, introduce biometric passports, take effective measures on illegal human and drug trafficking across its borders, and harmonize its current laws with the readmission and asylum policies of the EU.[39] The reform process had the same dysfunctional structure as in the police reform, where European Union dictated the conditions of the reform that BiH officials needed to achieve. In other reform areas, the demands of the EU accession process led to a further rift between nationalist politicians. However, contrary to experience, Bosnian politicians completed and implemented the conditions listed in the roadmap for visa liberalization without any major difficulty. The success of the visa liberalization process is a clear indication that Bosnian politicians are ready to play along on issues that are perceived as mutually beneficial to all three constituent nations in the country. Bosnian citizens are now able to travel freely to the Schengen zone as of December 2010.

Bosniak, Croat, and Serbian leaders have three different visions for the future direction and institutional restructuring of the country. The proposals brought to the table during the failed Butmir process in 2009 revealed three mutually exclusive perspectives. There was no state-level government in place several months after the October 2010 general elections. As a result, taking any further steps in the EU integration process has literally become impossible. One of the biggest obstacles that needs to be addressed once a state-level government is set up is the long-overdue harmonization of the Constitution with the December 2009 ruling of the European Court of Human Rights on the Sejdic-Finci case. ECHR found the State of Bosnia-Herzegovina guilty on grounds of ethnic discrimination regarding representation in the institutions of the country. The case was brought to the ECHR upon the request of Sejdic and Finci, both Bosnian citizens, respectively of Roma and Jewish origin, whose applications to run for the presidency were turned down by the Bosnian Electoral Board on the grounds that they did not belong to any of the three ethnic groups in the country. Noncompliance with the verdict might result in Bosnia's dismissal from the Council of Europe.

The EU accession process concentrates on the development of strong state-level institutions that are able to carry out the implementation of the adopted reforms in the sectors of police, education, media, and the transition to a liberal market economy. But the current consociational structure of the country and unsettled nationalist sentiments make the EU reform process a duel between the pro-centralization Bosniak leaderships and the pro-autonomy RS government. The joint desire for EU membership repeatedly voiced by political leaders remains at best rhetorical.

The EU policy in BiH is based on the assumption that conditionalities embedded in the accession process carry a transformative power, as the experience with the recent enlargement to the former socialist countries of Central and Eastern Europe has shown. Conditionalities implemented during the accession negotiations transformed these authoritarian political regimes with centrally planned socialist economic systems into pluralist liberal democracies with functioning, globally integrated market economies. The process with BiH has not gone as easily in conrast with the case of CEECs (Central and Eastern European Countries). Lessons learned from the recent expansion do not apply to BiH since none of

these countries had their national sovereignties divided between two politically powerful entities and three constituent nations with remarkably
little executive power vested in state-level institutions.

The EU presence in BiH is not limited to the community pillar. Bosnia-
Herzegovina has become a test case for Bosnia to evaluate its own security and defense capabilities. The European Police Mission (EUPM) in
Bosnia and the European Union Force (EUFOR)—Althea, are the two
missions that represent the current stage of the EU's efforts to develop its
own security and defense capacity. The next chapter examines the perfor-
mances of the two missions so far and their contributions to the security
situation in postconflict Bosnia.

NOTES

1. The delegation of the EU Troika consisted of foreign ministers of three countries: Hans van den Broek (Netherlands), Jacques Poos (Luxembourg), and João de
Deus Pinheiro (Portugal). The Troika consisted of the former, current, and future
holders of the rotating EU Presidency. The Lisbon Treaty amended the Troika substi-
tuting it with the permanent post of President of the Council, and the merger of the
posts of High Representative and External Relations Commissioner, as well as a
foreign action service of its own for the new EU Foreign Affairs post.

2. The European Community sponsored the signing of the Brioni Agreement on
July 7, 1991, by representatives of the Republic of Slovenia, Republic of Croatia, and
the Socialist Federal Republic of Yugoslavia. The text of the Agreement is available at
http://www.ucdp.uu.se/gpdatabase/peace/Yug percent2019910712.pdf.

3. It is also argued that the plan failed due to the lack of coercive measures to
compel the parties to an agreement, as well as the lack of pressure by the United
States.

4. Both the UNSCR 757 (1992) on 30 May 1992, imposing comprehensive sanctions
on the FRY, available at http://www.nato.int/ifor/un/u920530a.htm and UNSCR 821 of
April 17, 1993, available at http://www.nato.int/ifor/un/u930417a.htm, depended on
the commitment of European countries to impose trade restrictions on the neighbors
of BiH so that arms would not be received by any of the warring factions.

5. France and the UK were the main contributors to this operation. They provided
approximately one-third of the troops of UNPROFOR: 8,700 troops (6,200 French) out
of a total of 24,000 blue helmets from thirty-four countries (Gnesotto 2004). Available
at http://aei.pitt.edu/466/01/chai14e.html.

6. The possibility of forming a common EU foreign policy within the contact
group in the face of the tragedy in Bosnia was based on the presumed impact such a
common position could make considering that the UK held the EU presidency, Germany held the presidency of the OSCE, and France (like the UK) was a permanent
member of the UN Security Council.

7. In spite of that, in the last period of the conflict, the EU was able to deploy a
significant and innovative operation with the administration of Mostar.

8. The EU Council Summit in Madrid held on December 15–16, 1995, conclusions are available at http://ue.eu.int/ueDocs/cms_Data/docs/pressdata/en/ec/00400–C.EN 5.htm.

9. The Obnova and Phare programs added to an amount of €890.7 million by the end of 2000. In addition, the EU member states contributed over €1 billion in assistance between 1996 and 1999 to Bosnia-Herzegovina. Further info is available at http://www.southeasteurope.org/documents/assist_b_h.pdf.

10. The regional approach was adopted at the EU Council Meeting on February 26, 1996. Available at http://www.consilium.europa.eu/ueDocs/cms_Data/docs/pressdata/en/gena/028a0001.htm.

11. At their meeting of 29 April 1997, the General Affairs Council agreed to adopt a coherent and transparent policy toward Southeastern Europe. It is directed at four of the successor republics of the Former Yugoslavia (Croatia, Bosnia-Herzegovina, FRY, and FYROM), as well as Albania. The policy lays out clear conditions that these countries must fulfill in order to qualify for trade, aid, and deepening of relations with the EU. "Compte tenu de ce qui précède, l'UE est convenue de définir, dans le cadre de l'approche régionale, les conditions politiques et économiques qui constitueront le fondement d'une politique cohérente et transparente en ce qui concerne le développement de relations bilatérales dans le domaine des échanges commerciaux, de l'aide financière et de la coopération économique, ainsi que des relations contractuelles, en tenant compte du degré de souplesse qui s'impose. La stratégie de l'UE devrait encourager les pays concernés à remplir ces conditions, et non les en empêcher." Available at http://www.consilium.europa.eu/ueDocs/cms_Data/docs/pressdata/en/gena/028a0 057.htm.

12. For further information on the conclusion of the Vienna Summit of the EU Council of Presidents on December 11–12, 1998, please see http://ue.eu.int/ueDocs/cms_Data/docs/pressData/en/ec/00300–R1.EN8.htm.

13. A scanned version of the European Commission to European Council and European Parliament on Stabilization and Association Agreements for five countries of Southeastern Europe including Bosnia-Herzegovina is available at http://aei.pitt.edu/3571/01/000722_1.pdf.

14. Between 1996 and 2003, the amount of financial assistance provided to BiH authorities from the community budget adds up to a figure of €1,3434.73 million (figures available at http://www.delbih.ec.europa.eu/en/eu_and_country/issues2.htm).

15. The presidency conclusions of Santa Maria de Feira Summit held on June 19–20, 2000, are available at http://ue.eu.int/ueDocs/cms_Data/docs/pressData/en/ec/00200 –r1.en0.htm.

16. Conclusions of the November 24, 2000, Zagreb Summit are available at http://ec.europa.eu/enlargement/enlargement_process/accession_process/how_does_a_country_join_the_eu/sap/zagreb_summit_en.htm.

17. The Council Regulation related to the CARDS program is available at http://ec.europa.eu/enlargement/pdf/financial_assistance/cards/general/2666_00_en.pdf .

18. Text of the EU-Western Balkans Thessaloniki Summit Declaration on June 21, 2003, is available at http://ec.europa.eu/enlargement/enlargement_process/accession_process/how_does_a_country_join_the_eu/sap/thessaloniki_summit_en.htm.

19. Figures are available at http://www.delbih.ec.europa.eu/?akcija=clanak&CID=22&jezik=2&LID=32.

20. Available at http://www.delbih.ec.europa.eu/?akcija=clanak&CID=23&jezik=2&LID=33.

21. Further details are available at

22. Consultative Task Force (CTF) was established in 1998 as a joint vehicle for political dialogue and expert advice. Meetings of the CTF have constituted a central forum for technical and political exchanges. In 2006 the CTF was renamed Reform Process Monitoring (RPM).

23. One of the requirements, which is still not completed, is the reform of the Public Broadcasting System (PBS), one of the key European partnership priorities. Available at http://www.europa-eu-un.org/articles/en/article_1622_en.htm

24. The EU makes use of the sources of its member states in its indirect assistance to state-building in Bosnia-Herzegovina. The Danish School of Public Administration provides funding for capacity enhancement of the Directorate for European Integration, available at http://www.dfhnet.dk/service percent20elementer/english/international_projects/european_integration.aspx.

25. The feasibility study is available at http://eurlex.europa.eu/smartapi/cgi/sga_doc?smartapi!celexplus!prod!CELEXnumdoc&lg=en&numdoc=503DC0692.

26. Council Decision 2004/515/EC of June 14, 2004, on the principles, priorities, and conditions contained in the European Partnership with Bosnia-Herzegovina (OJ L 221, 22.6.2004, p. 10).

27. For Regulation (EC) No 533/2004, please see http://eur-lex.europa.eu/LexUriServ/site/en/consleg/2004/R/02004R0533–20060220–en.pdf.

28. The main priorities identified for Bosnia-Herzegovina relate to its capacity to meet the criteria defined by the Copenhagen European Council of 1993 and the conditions set for the Stabilization and Association Process, notably the conditions defined by the Council in its conclusions of April 29, 1997 and June 21–22, 1999, the content of the final declaration of the Zagreb Summit of 24 November 2000, and the Thessaloniki Summit in June 21, 2003.

29. Failure to respect these conditions could lead the Council to take appropriate measures on the basis of Article 5 of Regulation (EC) No 2666/2000 "Community assistance shall also be subject to the conditions defined by the Council in its conclusions of April 29, 1997, and June 21–22, 1999 in particular as regards the recipients' undertaking to carry out democratic, economic and institutional reforms."

30. Indeed, in an interview in May 2007, the General Secretary of the ruling SNSD, Rajko Vasic, indicated that the RS political leadership does not see a reason to compromise on the issue of police reform since EU membership did not look near and easy to achieve and maybe not even possible.

31. Available at http://www.ohr.int/ohr-dept/rule-of-law-pillar/prc/prc-keydoc/default.asp?content_id=36200.

32. In September 2005, the International Crisis Group (ICG) published a report on Bosnia titled "Bosnia's Stalled Police Reform: No Progress, No EU." This document is available at http://www.crisisgroup.org/library/documents/europe/balkans/164_bosnia_stalled_police_reform_no_progress_no_eu.pdf.

33. Slobodan Vaskovic, editor-in-chief of the Banja Luka weekly *Patriot*, received telephone threats on May 29, 2004. An unidentified voice allegedly said, "You and your family, and your paper will fly up in the air in the next 24 hours if you don't leave the Republika Srpska instantly" (taken from the BiH report of the 2004 World Press Freedom Review By South East Europe Media Organization [SEEMO]. Available at http://service.cms.apa.at/cms/ipi/freedom_detail.html?country=/KW0001/KW0003/KW0052/&year=2004).

34. *Patriot* weekly magazine. #168, 9 May 2005.

35.   The Police Reform Directorate was established by the BiH Council of Ministers on 8 December 2005 following the Political Agreement on 5 October 2005 regarding Restructuring of Police Structures in BiH. Available at http://www.ohr.int/ohr-dept/rule-of-law-pillar/prc/.

The Directorate has been tasked with exploring options on how to make the implementation of the reform possible that is acceptable to all the parties involved (for further details on the composition of the directorate see http://www.eupm.org/Documents/DPRI/Decision percent20Establishing percent20the percent20Directorate percent20for percent20Police percent20Restructuring percent20Implementation percent20ENG.doc).

36.   The EU Special Rep and HR Schwartz Schilling celebrated the conclusion of the report and urged the acceptance of the report by Council of Ministers by March 2007 (see http://www.ohr.int/ohr-dept/presso/pressr/default.asp?content_id=38773)/.

37.   "If we will have to choose between the European Union and the police of Republika Srpska, we will choose the police of Republika Srpska" (see RSPM Milorad Dodik's comments in an interview published on October 31, 2006, available at http://www.bosnia.org.uk/news/news_body.cfm?newsid=2235).

38.   By the end of 2011 the EU Special Representative is also going to be the head of the EU Commission Delegation. This move aims to bring more political muscle to the Commission Delegation.

39.   Roadmap for visa liberalization in Bosnia-Herzegovina is available at http://www.europa.ba/docs/map.pdf.

FIVE

The European Union's Crisis Management Mechanisms

This chapter analyzes the development of the EU's military and civilian crisis management concepts and evaluates the performance of the European Union Police Mission (EUPM) and the European Union Force (EUFOR) Althea Mission in BiH as the first practical extensions of these two concepts. The European Union intended to improve its crisis management competencies ever since the failure of its early diplomatic efforts during the disintegration of Yugoslavia. The EU peacemaking efforts at the time failed due to the EU's lack of muscle over the parties. The experiment in Bosnia is one through which the European Union expects to learn and roll out to other missions. The relatively stable security environment in Bosnia-Herzegovina provides a valuable and risk-free opportunity for the EU to assess the quality of its deliverables in peacebuilding. These deliverables are a number of hard security guarantees and on-site assistance that address outstanding challenges like the illegal drugs, arms and human trafficking through BiH, organized crime networks, and the search for war criminals.

THE EU'S MILITARY CRISIS MANAGEMENT CONCEPT

The Western European nations have maintained the desire for a separate security identity ever since the start of the Cold War. The former Western European Union (WEU) was such an attempt. The WEU was established by the Treaty on Economic, Social, and Cultural Collaboration and Collective Self-Defense signed at Brussels on March 17, 1948 (the Brussels Treaty) by Belgium, France, Luxembourg, the Netherlands, and the United Kingdom, as amended by the protocol signed in Paris on October 23, 1954, which modified and completed it. It was conceptualized as a response to the imposition of Soviet control over the Central European countries. The Brussels Treaty's basic premise was its commitment to mutual defense should any of the signatories fall victim to an attack in Europe. The Brussels Treaty also prompted the involvement of the United States in evolving European security frameworks. The eventual result of this engagement was the singing of the Washington Treaty in 1949, the North Atlantic Treaty Organization (NATO), which integrated Canada, Denmark, Iceland, Italy, Norway, and Portugal into the security framework and formalized the commitment of the US troops to the defense of Western Europe against a possible Soviet invasion from the east.[1] In 1950, the Brussels treaty signatories decided to merge their military competencies into NATO, which by then became the main component of the West European and North Atlantic security structure. In October 1950, France proposed the creation of a European Army under the NATO framework that would integrate West Germany into the emerging security structures. France's proposal led to the Treaty setting up a European Defense Community (EDC) in May 1952, which Belgium, France, Italy, Luxembourg, the Netherlands, and West Germany were expected to join. However, the refusal of the French National Assembly in August 1954 to ratify the Treaty postponed the plan for a unified European Army at least forty years. The Western European Union was created as an alternative to the failed EDC, with the goal of integrating West Germany and Italy into the North Atlantic and West European security frameworks. In September 1954, at a special conference in London, under the leadership of the UK and the US, West Germany and Italy were invited into the Brussels Treaty. In October 1954, the Paris Treaty amended the Brussels Treaty, creating the Western European Union (WEU) as a new international organization. The preamble of the amended Brussels treaty focused on three main objectives:

- To create a firm basis for European economic recovery in Western Europe;
- To afford assistance to each other in resisting any policy of aggression;

- To promote unity and encourage the progressive integration of Europe.[2]

Until 1973, the WEU played a pivotal role in generating cooperation and goodwill in Western Europe between the EC members and nonmembers like the UK. It helped facilitate the integration of West Germany in NATO; restored the confidence among Western European countries by gaining arms control responsibilities with the Agency for the Control of Armaments and the Standing Armaments Committee; managed the permanent settlement of the Saar problem between Germany and France; and served as a consultation mechanism between the EC founding members and the UK until it became a full member of the EC in 1973. The 1980s saw the expansion of the European Political Cooperation (EPC) into the security and defense pillars. The WEU has become a parallel platform for collaboration between the member states separate from European Economic Community (EEC) structures. The Rome Declaration on October 1984 set new goals for the WEU as an organization not only responsible for the security of Western Europe but also for the NATO members.

Following the end of the Cold War, the WEU began to take a more active role in conflict and crisis zones across the world. These activities included minesweeping duties in the Strait of Hormuz during the Iran-Iraq War and naval embargo coordination in the first Gulf War. WEU also helped coordinate humanitarian actions for Kurdish refugees in Northern Iraq. As a significant addendum to the NATO operations during the Yugoslav wars, the WEU contributed to the naval embargo against former Yugoslavia in the Adriatic Sea. Similarly, the WEU conducted joint reconnaissance missions with the OSCE in the Danube river basin countries of Hungary, Romania, and Bulgaria to support the arms embargo on Yugoslavia. WEU also contributed police contingents to the EU administration in the city of Mostar in the summer of 1994 for two years. The WEU also participated in police training activities in Albania (1997–2001), provided demining support in Croatia (1999–2001), and conducted general security surveillance in Kosovo (1998–1999).

EUROPEAN SECURITY AND DEFENSE POLICY (ESDP)

The negative experience during the Yugoslav wars in the nineties led the Europeans to question the effectiveness of the WEU and look for ways to develop a more robust defense policy. The NATO interventions to Yugoslavia revealed three facts. First, the inevitable American strategic and operational leadership in NATO operations in the European mainland created unease among pro-European circles in France and Germany. These circles began to argue that unless Europe began to develop and implement its own defense and security strategy and policies, it would remain dependent on US intervention and therefore lack any political credibility in the international scene. Second, whilst the European governments spent two-thirds as much as the US on defense, they managed to deploy only 10 percent as many troops to conflict regions (Forster and Wallace 2000, 481–485). If the EU were to be an effective military actor, the operational effectiveness needed to be harmonized with the budgetary allocations; otherwise, there would not be any robust and integrated financial foundation on which to build its security and defense policies. Third, the successful cooperation between the European nations under the NATO's Implementation Force (IFOR) and Stabilization Force (SFOR) in BiH raised hopes that a European military alliance could be achieved in the long run. At the Franco-British Summit in St. Malo in December 1998, the EU called for the strengthening of the Common Foreign and Security Policy (CFSP) through the creation of a European Security and Defense Policy (ESDP), renamed Common Security and Defense Policy (CSDP) after the Treaty of Lisbon in 2009.

Three European Council meetings set out the main guidelines of the ESDP. The Cologne Summit in June 1999 issued a declaration, "On Strengthening the Common European Policy on Security and Defense" stating that the European Union should have the ability to make decisions on the full range of conflict prevention and crisis management tasks defined in the Treaty on European Union, the 'Petersberg' tasks (European Council 1999a, Appendix III).[3] The Petersberg tasks are a list of military and security priorities incorporated within the former European Security and Defense Policy of the European Union. They include peacekeeping and peacemaking tasks that the European Union (EU) and the Western European Union (WEU) were empowered to do. The Amsterdam Treaty in 1997 already incorporated these tasks in the Treaty of the

European Union. The 1999 Cologne Summit transferred the WEU assets to the EU under the ESDP framework, making the distinction artificial.

The declaration emphasized the need for the EU to develop the capacity for autonomous action with credible military forces, courage, and willingness to use them in order to respond to international crises. During the following years, significant steps have were taken in order to move forward with the strengthening of the military crisis management. At the end of 2002, an agreement was reached on consultation mechanisms between the EU-ESDP and NATO; the Berlin-plus agreement gave the EU access to NATO assets and facilities (Haine 2003, Quille and Mawdsley 2003).[4] Moreover, an EU-led military operation that involved inter-institutional cooperation with access to NATO was successfully implemented in Macedonia (Operation Concordia). Operation Artemis ran independently of NATO in the Democratic Republic of Congo (DRC), and was conducted as an EU police mission in Bosnia as part of the civilian component of the ESDP (Monaco 2003). In 2003, the European Union negotiated a new constitution, first at the Constitutional Convention and then in an Inter-Governmental Conference. The strengthening of the ESDP was agreed upon at a special meeting of foreign ministers in Naples in November 2003. According to the final version of the EU Constitution, the Europeans would keep their operational headquarters within NATO and their potential crisis management campaigns explicitly subject to a NATO "right of first refusal."[5]

EU Defense Ministers agreed at their meeting on November 21, 2004, and adopted the Military Headline Goal 2010 to create thirteen "battle groups" by 2007, to be deployed to the world's hotspots. Battle groups are thought to be used in peacekeeping operations up to 6,000 kilometers away. The 1,000 to 1,500-strong forces are expected to be able to be quickly deployable. The forces were to be used under UN mandated operations, preparing the ground for bigger UN operations that take longer to deploy. The battle groups were also expected to take on smaller missions independently. Since January 2007, the EU has had two permanent battle groups on standby for deployment (Major and Molling 2011). But they have not been tested so far due to the divergence of opinions among the EU member states on how to utilize the EU peacekeeping competencies. As the implementation of the battle groups concept remains on hold, the EUFOR Althea mission in Bosnia-Herzegovina continues to serve as a crucial testing ground for the operationalization of EU military capabilities with NATO assets. Below is a study of EUFOR Althea's performance since 2004.

EUFOR-ALTHEA

The EUFOR-Althea is considered to be part of a coherent EU strategy. It aims to make a significant contribution to the EU's political engagement in the country, and to the EU's civilian crisis management operations (EU Police Mission) and with an objective to facilitate BiH's further progress in the EU integration process. EUFOR-Althea mission launched its operations in December 2004 with 7,000 troops on the ground. EUFOR mission took over all the responsibilities of the NATO mission, Stabilization Force (SFOR). Through time, the number of troops gradually decreased. Since March 2007, all of the military camps besides the Butmir Camp near Sarajevo have been turned over to the command of the unified Bosnian Army.[6] The number of troops in the Multinational Maneuver Battalion (MNBN) in the Butmir Camp, near Sarajevo has been reduced to around 1,500 including the Liaison Observation Teams (LOTs) spread throughout in the country. Currently twenty-six nations contribute troops, including twenty-one EU Member States and five non-EU Nations. These troops leverage the critical operational capabilities to carry out EUFOR's Chapter VII mission. Chapter VII of the UN Charter gives authority for the use of force in peacekeeping missions when faced with a threat to human lives, indicating that impartiality does not mean neutrality in cases of crimes against humanity[7] :

- To provide deterrence and continued compliance with the responsibility to fulfill the role specified in Annexes 1A and 2 of the Dayton/Paris Agreement (General Framework Agreement for Peace in BiH); and
- To contribute to a safe and secure environment in BiH, in line with its mandate, and to achieve core tasks in the OHR's Mission Implementation Plan and the Stabilization and Association Process (SAP).[8]

The key supporting tasks of the Althea mission include operational support to the International Criminal Tribunal for the Former Yugoslavia (ICTY) and relevant authorities, such as the detention of PIFWCs, and ensuring the security environment in which the police can act against the organized criminal networks.

ABSENCE OF A SUBSTANTIAL MILITARY THREAT: SUCCESS OF THE DEFENSE REFORM

The transfer of the military bases to the Bosnian Army is an achievement that was not possible to imagine at the beginning of the decade without NATO's constructive engagement in the defense reform process. Defense reform mainly aimed to establish democratic control over the armed forces. The destruction of the war in BiH, and in the former Yugoslavia are, to a certain extent, consequences of what happens when the armed forces of a country are reduced to a political tool in the hands of ethno-nationalism. The OHR Mission Implementation plan, established in 2003, clearly sets security sector reform as one of the core tasks of the international community to make BiH a functioning state. "Establishing State-level civilian command and control over armed forces, and reform of the security sector" is underlined as the path for the Euro-Atlantic integration.[9]

The international community's focus on strengthening the state-level institutions shapes the scope of the defense reform. The defense reform essentially aimed to set up a state-level Ministry of Defense with executive powers and reduce the size of the armed forces in both entities in order to create a unified professional Bosnian army. Implementation of the reform necessitated the abolishment of the entity-level armies and an end to the conscription system. All throughout the reform process, the NATO task force, embedded in the state-level Ministry of Defense, provided constant assistance and cooperated with the Bosnian authorities.[10] On December 14, 2006, eleven years after the Dayton Peace Agreement, Bosnia Herzegovina signed the Partnership for Peace (PfP) Agreement with NATO. This agreement made BiH a future NATO member and redefined its international security within the framework of the Euro-Atlantic cooperation.[11] The next step in the NATO integration was the signing of the Membership Action Plan (MAP). It took more than three years for BiH to be officially invited into the MAP by NATO.

Countries participating in the MAP are asked to submit individual annual national programs on their preparations for possible future membership. These cover political, economic, defense, resource, security, and legal aspects. The MAP process provides a focused and candid feedback mechanism on aspirant countries' progress on their programs. This includes both political and technical advice, as well as annual meetings between all NATO members and individual aspirants at the level of the North Atlantic Council to assess progress. A key element is the defense planning approach for aspirants, which includes elaboration and review of agreed planning targets.[12]

In April 2010, NATO invited BiH into the Membership Action Plan (MAP) on the condition that it resolves its defense property issue. The ongoing dispute between the RS political leadership and the FBiH about the reallocation of the defense properties to the state-level keeps Bosnia out of MAP.

EUFOR'S PSYCHOLOGICAL MANDATE

The deterrence function of the EUFOR against conventional military threats has become largely irrelevant.[13] The decision of the European Council for General Affairs and External Relations recognized this and reduced the number of troops in March 2007. Annex 1A (Military Aspects of the Peace Settlement) and Annex 2 (Inter-Entity Boundary Line and Related Issues) of the Dayton Peace Agreement no longer apply to the contemporary security situation in Bosnia, especially after the signing of the PfP agreement and invitation to MAP.[14] The main function of EUFOR's presence in BiH is providing psychological reassurance as the country moves from the postconflict stage to the democratic transition phase. EUFOR-Althea mission is evolving in the direction of a nonexecutive operation, as has been pointed out in the joint report by Solana and Rehn in 2006.[15]

Figures in table 5.1 indicate that the Bosnian public does not see the renewal of violence as a possibility. The presence of the EUFOR troops

Table 5.1.   Do you think war might break out if the EUFOR withdraws? (data extracted from the UNDP 2010 Early Warning Report on BiH)

	Bosniaks		Croats		Serbs	
	Nov-09	Nov-10	Nov-09	Nov-10	Nov-09	Nov-10
Yes	35.9	22.6	15.3	2.9	19.1	8
No	53.4	69.9	69.4	94.3	73.1	80.5

has a psychological deterrence function against any possible ethnic intimidation between radicals. Traditionally Bosniaks are the most risk-averse groups among the three constituent nations and thus the most supportive of the continuation of an international presence as a safeguard against Serbian irredentism. Even among the Bosniak sample the percentage of the pessimists was at an all-time low in November 2010.

According to the findings of the author's field interviews with Bosnian politicians and Bosnian civil society members, the EUFOR mission serves two main purposes. First is the psychological guarantees it provides for the long-term political stability of Bosnia. Although Bosnians see the resumption of the conflict as a distant possibility, the presence of EUFOR troops on the ground provides for such perceptions. It would be very interesting to see the results of a survey conducted on the possibility of a renewal of conflict after the withdrawal of EUFOR troops. Second, the Althea mission serves to prevent any spillovers from the political security dilemma into violence between factions. Most importantly, the EUFOR-Althea mission has helped the militaries of the participating nation states learn to operate under joint command structures and achieve oversight competencies in a postconflict country.[16]

A RISK-FREE ENVIRONMENT: DO NOT TOUCH KARADZIC AND MLADIC

One of the EUFOR's key support tasks has been to support the ICTY in the search for missing war criminals (PFWCs); the wartime president of Republika Srpska, Radovan Karadzic; and General Ratko Mladic, the wartime commander of the RS Army. EUFOR had the capability and mandate to search and arrest war criminals, and was tasked to act where Bosnian officials could not. Yet neither the NATO task force in BiH, the designated actor to conduct intelligence work on the whereabouts of the indicted war criminals, nor the EUFOR have taken any part in the capture of Karadzic and Mladic. This was a political decision from the start. An active pursuit and capture mission by the EUFOR would have carried a high political risk that the EUFOR-Althea was not willing to take. The EUFOR refrained from giving an impression of favoring Sarajevo's priorities over Banja Luka's. The two fugitives enjoyed significant popularity among the Bosnian Serbs. Second, both the European Union officials and the international community have preferred that the search of the PFWCs be conducted by local security authorities such as the Bosnian Intelligence Agency (SIPA) through their own means. Indeed, a EUFOR official interviewed in January 2006 at EUFOR's strategic headquarters in Mons, Belgium, indicated that it was the responsibility of the local authorities to catch war criminals and bring them to the ICTY.

Both Karadzic's and Mladic's capture operations were conducted by Serbia's elite security forces. Both of these figures are accused of crimes committed against humanity through the massacre of civilians during the three-year siege of Sarajevo and the Srebrenica genocide. The capture of Karadzic and Mladic has an emotional quality for the people of Bosnia-Herzegovina and the region, marking the end of the postwar era.

SAFE MISSIONS: OPERATION ILLEGAL LOGGING AND SPOTTING SECRET WEAPON STORAGES

EUFOR's crackdowns on illegal logging or spotting secret weapon storages have been examples of mission success in the fight against organized crime. Such actions, without any political risk, were deemed ideal to boost the credibility of the EUFOR. Given that the EU wanted to keep the EUFOR-Althea as politically neutral as possible, the mission has been a success. Supporting BiH's progress into the SAP through spontaneous operations against organized crime networks in BiH territories fits into the comprehensive approach of the EU in BiH. However, one should not forget that the EUFOR has not been yet tested in a real crisis situation. In such situations impartiality should not be confused with neutrality. The risk-free success of the Althea mission since 2004 has not yet managed to remove the dark image of the 'neutral' Dutch peacekeepers abandoning Srebrenica to the Serb paramilitaries in 1995.

WHAT SHOULD BE NEXT FOR EUFOR-ALTHEA?

The EUFOR-Althea has fulfilled its CH VII mandate to a large extent, and should phase out once Bosnia Herzegovina signs the Membership for Action Plan for NATO. The objectives of the new mission should be redefined as an assistance mission that provides hands-on guidance to Bosnian Armed Forces during their preparation for NATO membership. A delegation of military technical experts can continue to provide assistance in streamlining the command and operational structures. In the past decade, Bosnian troops gained international operational experience as part of a number of UN and NATO missions in Afghanistan, Iraq, and Sub-Saharan African countries. The next generation EUFOR assistance should facilitate the transfer of international know-how into the Bosnian Army's daily operational procedures.

The next section focuses on the EU's civilian crisis management capabilities and the performance of the EU Police Mission (EPM) in Bosnia.

THE EU'S CIVILIAN CRISIS MANAGEMENT COMPETENCIES

This section analyzes the development of the civilian crisis management competencies of the EU and evaluates the performance of the EUPM in BiH. In June 2000, the EU Council Summit in Feira, Portugal, declared EU's intentions to develop civilian crisis management competencies. The summit identified four priority areas: police, strengthening of the rule of law, strengthening civilian administration, and civil protection.[17] Under the priority area of police, it was agreed that member states would commit 5,000 civilian police officers to be deployed within thirty days to crisis situations. Since then, the EU has contributed to a number of police missions across the globe.[18]

The European Union Police Mission (EUPM)

The European Union Police Mission (EUPM) is one of the most ambitious attempts of the EU to test its civilian crisis management competencies in the area of rule of law. The EUPM I and II missions are parts of a broader effort undertaken by the EU and other actors to address the full range of rule of law aspects in BiH. In line with the general objectives of the Paris/Dayton Agreement, the EUPM sought to establish sustainable policing arrangements under Bosnian ownership. The EUPM's first assignment was launched on January 1, 2003, for an initial period of three years. In 2007 and 2009, the mission's mandate and size were modified and extended; the EUPM II mission is expected to last until the end of 2011. The mandate of the mission reads as follows:

> Under the direction of the EUSR, the EUPM coordinates the policing aspects of the European Security and Defense Policy (ESDP) efforts in the fight against organized crime and as part of the broader rule of law

approach in BiH and the region, aims through mentoring, monitoring, and inspecting to establish a sustainable, professional and multiethnic police service in BiH, operating in accordance with the best European and international standards. This police service should operate in accordance with commitments made as part of the Stabilization and Association Process with the European Union, in particular with regard to the fight against organized crime and police reform. It assists local authorities in planning and conducting major and organized crime investigations.[19]

In 2003, when the EU took over the police mission from the UN, it was argued that the immediate postconflict period was over and that the task of policing was to be transferred to local police structures. For that reason, the mandate of the EUPM was more political and focused on institution-building compared to its predecessor, the more technical and action-oriented International Police Task Force (IPTF) mission of the UN. The EUPM does not have an executive mandate. The IPTF had coercive and binding measures against organized crime that had much closer relations with the war criminals, some of whom were police officers. Hence, the presence of an international police force was considered necessary to unravel these relations. The police forces of both entities were either in the initial phase of their re-institutionalization, or most of their members were indicted with war crimes during the war. The IPTF was particularly helpful with its practical approach against the war criminals in police structures, and for its effective crackdown on organized crime networks.[20]

The EUPM operates in line with the general objectives of Annex 11 of the Dayton Agreement and is supported by European Community instruments.[21] The EUPM presence in BiH has three strategic components: supporting the local police in the fight against organized crime, increasing the accountability of local police, and providing support to the implementation of police restructuring.[22] The EUPM assistance through these strategic pillars aims to strengthen Bosnian ownership and set up functioning institutions for rule of law. Below is an analysis of the performance of the EUPM on each strategic pillar.

Support to Bosnian Police in the Fight against Organized Crime

The UN Convention against Transnational Organized Crime 2000 defines an organized criminal group as a "structured group of three or more persons, existing for a long period of time and acting in concert with the aim of committing one or more serious crimes or offences . . . in order to obtain, directly or indirectly, a financial or other material benefit" (United Nations 2000, Art. 2). According to the document, a structured group is "a group that is not randomly formed . . . and that does not need to have formally defined roles for its members, continuity for its membership or a developed structure."[23] Organized crime involves trafficking of drugs and people, extortion, kidnapping for profit, environmental crime such as illegal toxic waste dumping, "sophisticated" credit card fraud, smuggling to evade excise tax on alcohol and tobacco, intellectual copyright theft, and corruption to achieve these offences (Levi 2002, 880). The practice of organized crime in the Western Balkans has a *transnational* or *cross-border* characteristic. Article 3(2) of the UN Convention argues that an offense becomes transnational when it is

> (i) committed in more than one state, (ii) committed in one state but prepared/planned/directed/controlled in another state, (iii) committed in one state but involves an organized criminal group that engages in criminal activities in more than one state, or (iv) if it is committed in one state but has substantial effects in another state.[24]

BiH sits on one of the busy crossroads for drug and human trafficking between Central Europe and the Middle East. According to the 2010 World Report of the UN Office on Drug and Crime (UNODC), the Balkan route traverses the Islamic Republic of Iran (often via Pakistan), Turkey, Greece, and Bulgaria across south-east Europe to the western European market, with an annual market value of some $20 billion.[25] The local organized crime networks have their operations integrated with the transnational networks and receive substantial financial benefits as a result. According to the US State Department's 2011 International Narcotics Control Strategy Report (INCSR), there is "mounting evidence of links and conflict among Bosnian criminal elements and organized crime operations in Russia, Albania, Serbia, Montenegro, Croatia, Austria, Germany, Italy, and increasingly even South American criminal networks."[26] Bosnia is not considered a significant narcotics producer, consumer, or producer of precursor chemicals. Bosnian officials' fight against drug trafficking is marked by "weak state institutions, lack of personnel in counternarcotics units, and limited cooperation among the responsible authorities contribute to Bosnia's vulnerability to narcotic trafficking."[27]

BiH lacks comprehensive antinarcotics intelligence and enforcement capabilities. The EU supports the strengthening of state-level law enforcement institutions such as the Border Police (BP) and State Investigative and Protection Agency (SIPA) through donations of critical high-tech surveillance equipment by individual member states. BiH has eighty-nine international border crossings on a 1,551 kilometer-long land border. Border patrol service is one of the better functioning law enforcement bodies in the country. However, the declining relative wages, vis-à-vis other local and entity law enforcement agencies, and harsh working conditions have led to sustained staff shortages in the BP. There are still a large number of illegal crossing points, including rural roads and river fords, where the BP lacks the manpower to patrol regularly. Moreover, many official checkpoints and many crossings remain understaffed. SIPA aspires to be a catalyst for information and evidence exchange between local and international law enforcement agencies, however, cooperation between local law enforcement agencies and SIPA is often less than optimal. The state-level Ministry of Security has created a Counter-narcotics Office in its Sector for the Suppression of Serious Narcotics Crimes. Although this office has the mandate to collect and disseminate drug-related data, its work is hindered by the occasional refusal of local law enforcement agencies to share information with it. Cooperation among law enforcement agencies and prosecutors is largely informal. There are still ad hoc and serious legal and bureaucratic obstacles to the effective prosecution of criminals.

Bosnia-Herzegovina is also a source, destination, and transit country for men, women, and children who are subjected to sex trafficking and forced labor. Bosnian victims are subjected to sex trafficking and forced labor in Azerbaijan, Slovenia, Croatia, and other countries in Europe. According to the US State Department's 2011 Trafficking of Humans Report, there were continued anecdotal reports of police and other officials' facilitation of trafficking, including by willfully ignoring, exploiting trafficking victims, and actively protecting traffickers or exploiters of trafficking victims in return for payoffs.[28]

The EUPM aims to build the operational capacity of the Bosnian police force through providing on-site mentoring, monitoring, and advisory support on the daily operations of the police. The new state-level security institutions, like the State Investigation and Protection Agency (SIPA), Ministry of Security (MoS), and the State Border Service (SBS) need the backing of the EUPM to leverage their own operational capacity to fight against the organized crime networks effectively. The on-site EUPM officers provide operational advice and support in planning and conducting investigations and operations against organized crime. However, the EUPM does not have an executive mandate and is not keen on guarding the Bosnian borders, which could be considered counterintuitive to the overall goal of strengthening the local policing capacity.

The EUPM officers monitor and provide on-demand training for the effective use of the high-tech surveillance equipment donated by the EU member states. EUPM has provided active knowledge management and operational support to the State Border Service on the set goals required for the visa liberalization agreement with the EU. The EUPM assistance has facilitated the implementation of a number of border security improvement projects. The EUPM Border Police also guides the BiH Border Police to fulfill the requirements set forth by the Integrated Border Management. This is a complex task that encompasses the whole field of border control and all agencies involved in this task—Border Police, Indirect Taxation Agency, Service for Foreigners' Affairs, Phytosanitary Control, and Veterinary Control.[29]

Strengthening the Accountability of Bosnian Police

Accountability and integrity of the Bosnian police is damaged by allegations of corruption and violation of human rights in the direction of everyday policing. According to Kutnjak Ivkovic and Shelley (2005), a police agency of low integrity is one in which police officers do not resist temptations of their office and engage in serious forms of police misconduct. Such police agencies serve the agency's or individual members' own interests, or the interests of those who are willing and can afford to buy their services. A corrupt police force is one that lacks transparency and is definitely not held accountable to the rule of law. It is not concerned with the protection of human rights in the process. In a recent survey conducted by the UNDP in 2010, 83 percent of Bosnian citizens believe that the Bosnian police is corrupt (bribery or abuse of office for private purposes) to varying degrees.[30]

Perception of corruption is widespread among the police units. The analysis by Maljevic and colleagues (2006) of a corruption survey conducted on 742 police officers from the Federation, RS, and the Brcko District revealed that 51 percent of officers stated that they either knew about cases of fraud in the police or they had accepted a bribe. In the same survey, many officers (especially older officers and officers working in the RS) reported dissatisfaction with the incompetent government and police efforts to locate and fight against corruption. The IPTF established Professional Standards Units (PSUs) in most Federation police agencies (and the Brcko police) to conduct investigations on alleged internal corruption/misconduct cases and submit confirmed cases to police disciplinary committees. Nonetheless, the effectiveness of the PSUs is largely curtailed due to political meddling, preferential treatment in disciplinary action, and senior police commissioners discounting the findings of the reports (ICG 2002; Palmer 2004). Similarly in the RS, investigation of police corruption is conducted by the Crime Investigations Police Department under the RS Ministry of Internal Affairs, which is subject to constant political pressure (Maljevic et al. 2006). At this time, it is not possible to determine the success of this unit in combating police corruption.

EUPM intervention aims to increase the integrity level of the Bosnian police through on-site inspections and daily monitoring of police operations from its initial planning stages, through investigations or operations, until the case in question reaches court. The EUPM officers monitor the situation inside the police—situations that are perceived as illegal, negligence, or contrary to the best practice or general rules of engagement. The EUPM has the right of free access to every document, premises or person to carry out this task. Embedded EUPM officers are intended to keep a close eye on the interactions of Bosnian police officers with the public and politicians.

There are two major challenges for the EUPM on this pillar. The EUPM officers' average tenure in Bosnia-Herzegovina does not outlast the six- to twelve-month bracket. Most of the EUPM operational officers are seconded from their home countries for a limited period, and have to move back to their home countries just around the time they finally familiarize themselves with the conduct of the Bosnian police. The new batch of officers arriving has to go through a similar learning curve until they also depart. This poses a significant challenge to maintaining a high-level knowledge management and operational capacity to carry out effective support for the Bosnian police in curtailing corruption. Corruption is not an easily observable phenomenon; it is disguised within daily operational police activities. It would require a familiarization period with the existing professional culture. Almost all of the seconded EUPM officers use English as their means of communication with Bosnian police officers, and in some cases, they have to employ the use of a translator to provide mentoring and advisory services.[31] Inevitably various nuances that would suggest misconduct get lost in translation, or are gone unnoticed due to language and culture barriers.

The EU Police Mission has a number of operational strengths that make the mission highly critical for the visibility of the European Union as an actor of peace in the country. The EUPM's most obvious strength lies in its unconditional support to capacity building efforts of the Bosnian police. Contrary to the conditionality clause embedded in the EU accession process, the EU police mission provides knowledge transfer and operational support regardless of the progress made by the Bosnian police. The Civilian Planning and Conduct Capability (CPCC) in Brussels[32] has realized that supporting the fight against organized crime in BiH is actually the fight against organized crime in Western Europe considering the transnational nature of drug and human trafficking through the Balkan route (Merlingen and Ostrauskaite 2008). The nonintrusive but consistent support to the strengthening of police structures makes the EUPM the most popular international mission in the Bosnian public opinion.[33] The respect for local ownership is definitely needed for the long-term sustainable fight against organized crime by local police structures. During the failed police reform process, EUPM officials demonstrated a sophisticated degree of flexibility in building a politically neutral picture but still acted as an advisory body to all the ethnic groups by establishing the Police Steering Board and cochairing it with the local authorities.

One obvious shortcoming of the EUPM I from 2003 until 2007 was its inability to share intelligence with Bosnian officials since BiH had not signed a strategic cooperation agreement with the European Law Enforcement Organization (EUROPOL). Trans-border crime cannot be fought in an isolated manner. EUROPOL aims at improving the effectiveness and co-operation of the competent authorities in EU member states and nonmembers in preventing and combating terrorism, illegal drug trafficking, and other serious forms of international organized crime. One Bosnian police officer interviewed in April of 2006 from the state-level Ministry of Security (MoS) indicated that lack of a formal strategic agreement between BiH and the EUROPOL significantly hampered the emergence of real cooperation between the BiH police authorities and the EUPM in launching a successful campaign against criminal networks.

EUROPOL signs strategic agreements with countries that are judged to offer an inadequate level of data protection. Under the Strategic Agreement, operational cooperation is somewhat limited; "although the partner may provide any information of preference to EUROPOL, EUROPOL may not give any personal information in return" (Brown 2008, 64). After the signing of the Strategic Agreement with EUROPOL in January 2007, the start of a limited sharing of intelligence between the EUPM and Bosnian police structures has had a positive impact on the success of organized crime network investigations.[34] An Operational Cooperation Agreement with EUROPOL remains to be completed due to lack of implementation of police reform that would establish an integrated police structure for all of BiH.[35]

EUSR

Until very recently, the European Union Special Representative (EUSR) has been a subsidiary office represented by the High Representative. The High Representatives to date have all been from European Union member states, in order to underline European responsibility for Bosnia Herzegovina. Officially, the EUSR ensures "a coordinated and coherent EU approach" to help BiH "move beyond peace implementation towards European Union integration."[36] This formal definition recognizes the transitional character of Bosnian politics and tasks the EUSR with integrating crisis management and community competencies. Tasks of the EUSR include:

- Offering the European Union's advice and facilitation to support political processes, including, in particular, the constitutional-reform process;
- Promoting overall EU political coordination, reinforcing internal EU coordination and coherence, and ensuring consistency and coherence of EU action;
- Giving local political guidance to both EUFOR and the EU Police Mission; monitoring rule-of-law activities and providing EU institutions with advice on this issue;

- Supporting the preparation and implementation of police restructuring and providing support for a reinforced and more effective criminal justice system;
- Engaging with relevant local authorities to achieve their full cooperation with the International Criminal Tribunal for the former Yugoslavia (ICTY); and
- Contributing to the development and consolidation of respect for human rights and fundamental freedoms.[37]

The tasks of the EUSR are both political and operational. EUSR has a limited version of the OHR's mandate that only assesses the performance of the EU institutions in BiH.[38] By regulating the performance of the EU's military and civilian crisis instruments in BiH, the EUSR is thought to help BiH politicians achieve progress in implementing the Dayton Peace Agreement as well as in the Stabilization and Association Process. The EUSR has some deficits that deserve recognition.

EUSR has set a very ambitious goal of providing political assistance to BiH leaders as the country struggles to complete the necessary reforms. The High Representative (until very recently the same person) has already been tasked with executive powers to enable Bosnia's political transition. But the experience of the past fifteen years shows that without securing the commitment of Bosnian politicians, the powers of the OHR are useless. Without similar political leverage over Bosnian politicians, the mandate of the EUSR does not specify how the EUSR is going to assist the transition by providing coordination to the activities of EU crisis management instruments. The EUSR is a crisis management instrument of the Council Secretariat. The European Union currently has nine Special Representatives "that promote European Union policies and interests in troubled regions and countries and play an active role in efforts to consolidate peace, stability and the rule of law."[39] In its former setup, the EUSR was not able to integrate the EU policies in BiH.

This book identifies the EU accession perspective as the most significant policy tool of the EU that needs to be supported by the crisis management instruments. The crisis instruments of the EU by themselves do guarantee the physical security of the country, as well as provide assistance in the setting up and running of institutions thought to provide "clean air" for liberal democracy to flourish in BiH. The EU membership perspective, on the other hand, as has been argued many times by the European Commission officials and EU-affiliated researchers, is intended to replace the "push of the international community" with the "pull of the European Union." The current state of affairs in BiH can hardly be considered as encouraging since neither political pressure by the OHR nor the possibility of becoming a EU Candidate Country has so far managed to weaken the authoritarian status quo in BiH that generates successive political crises. Furthermore, as one European Commission Official interviewed in Brussels in January 2006 noted, the presence of the EUSR in a future EU candidate is not a good omen for the political stability of that country.

The new EUSR Office will be an independent body from the OHR, also acting as the Head of the Delegation of the EU in BiH. Such an arrangement is in line with the Lisbon Treaty, where the General Secretary of the Council Secretariat becomes the vice president of the European Commission. With such an arrangement, the Special Representative could exploit the membership perspective as a real policy tool that could help BiH politicians realize that, without genuine attempts for reform, BiH would remain a claustrophobic environment trapped in its postconflict, ethno-political arrangement. Under the current composition of the EU institutions, the Commission Delegation is an implementer of and reporter to the European Commission in Brussels. The functional design of the Delegation is of a passive observer of political developments in the country to provide feedback on the progress of BiH to the relevant DGs in Brussels. The fact that the membership perspective, being the most powerful and essential tool of the EU in BiH, is regulated only through such a passive, bureaucratic organization like the European Commission, is a serious blow to the effectiveness of the EU as a peace actor in BiH. The Special Representative should also be empowered to determine whether the delivery of the reconstruction and development funds (pre-accession funds, IPA) is decreased or stopped in case of political obstruction by BiH politicians. This new arrangement would be much more effective than threatening to put the SAP on hold in case of failure of implementation of reforms.

CONCLUSION

In this chapter we analyzed the development process of the European Union's crisis management competencies as a distinct identity from the existing North Atlantic security frameworks. Postconflict Bosnia-Herzegovina has provided an ideal testing ground for the implementation of the EU crisis management mechanisms on a substantial scale. The EUFOR-Althea's presence still serves as a psychological safeguard of the international community against any risk of renewal of ethnic conflict. The EUFOR officials pay particular attention to remaining politically neutral. For that reason, the EUFOR-Althea did not launch any active duty missions to seek and capture PIFWCs Karadzic and Mladic, to avoid alienating the Bosnian Serbs among which Karadzic and Mladic still enjoyed considerable popularity. The near completion of the defense reform has also eased the tasks of the EUFOR Liaison Observation Teams spread across the country. Bosnian Army has been united into a 10,000 strong professional body, the RS Army has been disbanded, and the national conscription in the Federation has been discontinued. All these developments put BiH on a secure path to NATO membership although the issue of reallocation of the defense property to the state level remains to be resolved. The EUFOR-Althea mission gradually needs to phase out its operational focus from a CH VII peacekeeping mission. A much smaller sized military assistance contingency in the Bosnian Army HQ in Sarajevo could provide advice and guidance to the Bosnian Army on its path to NATO membership.

EU's Police Mission, on the other hand, has been significantly effective in generating the operational capacity of the nascent Bosnian state-level police structures against unconventional security threats, such as transnational organized crime networks. Bosnia-Herzegovina sits on the crossroads of the historic Balkan route of human and drug trafficking into Western Europe. EUPM's refocused approach on on-site mentoring, monitoring, and advice has helped the mission build strong institutional links with the Bosnian state-level security institutions like SIPA, Ministry of Security, and State Border Service. The EUPM's unconditional operational and knowledge management support of Bosnian police structures makes it unique among other EU institutions in BiH whose policies are built around conditionalities. There are a number challenges to the EUPM, such as the language barrier where seconded police officers communicate in English with their counterparts in the Bosnian police agencies, and often through a translator. A substantial segment of the EUPM staff consists of these seconded police officers, whose average tenure in the mission doesn't outlast twelve months. Seconded EUPM officers return to their home countries around the time they get familiar with the

Bosnian police culture, a time critical to identifying corruption and politi-cal interference. This is a structural challenge to EUPM's assistance on the fight against corruption among the Bosnian police staff.

Both the EUPM and the EUFOR-Althea aim to support and facilitate Bosnia's EU accession process by minimizing the security risks while helping BiH generate its own security competencies. BiH is a risk-free, failure-proof testing ground for the EU military and civilian crisis man-agement competencies. Neither of these missions had to confront any serious security challenges that would defy their strategic capabilities. Although both EUPM and EUFOR have contributed to constructing a safe and secure environment in Bosnia, EU's most significant policy tool is still the membership perspective. The membership perspective pro-vides the overall framework for the crisis management activities.

The next chapter concludes the book by providing a list of factors that affect the EU's effectiveness in Bosnia.

NOTES

1. Article 5 of the NATO Treaty states that an armed attack against one of the signatories shall be considered an attack against them all and that each party will then take such action as it deems necessary to restore and maintain the security of the North Atlantic area.

2. Please see the Brussels Treaty's Preamble.

3. Petersberg tasks were defined in June 1992 at the Hotel Petersberg near Bonn in Germany at a meeting of the Council of the WEU, where the member states agreed to deploy their troops and resources from across the whole spectrum of the military under the authority of the WEU.

4. See the documents on these EU-NATO meetings and agreements, specifically the European Union-NATO declaration on ESDP, Brussels, December 16, 2002.

5. Available at http://euobs.com/?aid=13877&rk=1.

6. In 2007, EUFOR handed the army bases in Banja Luka, Tuzla, and Mostar to BiH military authorities. EUFOR concentrated its military power in the former Yugo-slav Air Base, Camp Butmir near Sarajevo. More information is available at http://www.euforbih.org/eufor/index.php?option=com_content&task=view&id=199&Item-id=1.

7. Further information is available at http://www.un.org/aboutun/charter/chap-ter7.htm.

8. The mission statement of EUFOR is available at www.euforbih.org.

9. Further details on the issue are available at http://www.ohr.int/ohr-info/ohr-mip/default.asp?content_id=29145.

10. Interview with Raffi Gregorian, the-then Head of the NATO Contingency in the Defense Ministry of BiH on June 14, 2006. Interview with an official from the US Embassy in Sarajevo on June 13, 2006.

11. The speech of the NATO Secretary General, Jaap de Hoop Scheffer, at the meeting of the Signing of the Partnership for Peace Framework Document by Bosnia-Herzegovina on December 14, 2006, emphasizes the strategic importance of the agreement for BiH. Please see http://www.nato.int/docu/speech/2006/s061214b.htm.

12. Membership Action Plan (MAP) definition is available at http://www.nato.int/cps/en/natolive/topics_37356.htm,

13. Similar arguments were put forward in the interview with the POLAD Officer from the European Union Force (EUFOR) in Bosnia-Herzegovina.

14. Available at http://www.ohr.int/dpa/default.asp?content_id=370.

15. Available at http://www.consilium.europa.eu/ueDocs/cms_Data/docs/pressData/en/reports/91339.pdf.

16. Out of fifteen Bosnian politicians and civil society representatives interviewed on the EUFOR mission between 2006 and 2010, nine indicated that EUFOR presence on the ground provides a psychological guarantee for long-term political stability, five suggested that the EUFOR prevents the spillover of the security dilemma to physical violence, and one argued that EUFOR facilitates Bosnia's NATO integration process.

17. Please see http://www.europarl.europa.eu/summits/fei2_en.htm#an1 for Annex I the Santa Maria Da Feira European Council Conclusions of the Presidency held on June 19–20, 2000.

18. Other policing missions include the EULEX (Kosovo), EUJUST LEX (Iraq), EUPOL COPPS (in the Palestinian Territories), EU BAM (at Rafah, Gaza), EU operations (in the Democratic Republic of the Congo), EUBAM (Moldova and Ukraine), EUPOL (Afghanistan), and EUMM (Georgia).

19. Available at http://www.eupm.org/Our percent20Mandate.aspx.

20. The ICG report on "Bosnia's Stalled Police Reform: No Progress, No EU" dated September 6, 2005, talks about the problems in transition from IPTF to EUPM is available   at   http://www.crisisgroup.org/library/documents/europe/balkans/164_bosnia_stalled_police_reform_no_progress_no_eu.pdf.

21. Annex 11 is available at http://www.nato.int/ifor/gfa/gfa-an11.htm.

22. The EUPM mission objectives are available at http://www.eupm.org/MissionObjectives.aspx.

23. Available at http://www.unodc.org/pdf/crime/a_res_55/res5525e.pdf.

24. Ibid.

25. One of the main routes for drug trafficking starts in Albania, continues through Montenegro, passes through Bosnia to Croatia and Slovenia, and then on to Central Europe. World Drug Report 2010 is available at http://www.unodc.org/unodc/en/data-and-analysis/WDR-2010.html.

26. The US State Department's 2011 International Narcotics Control Strategy Report is available at http://www.state.gov/p/inl/rls/nrcrpt/2011/vol1/156359.htm#bosnia andherzegovina.

27. Ibid.

28. In September 2010, the government suspended an investigation of seventeen individuals for charges including the sex trafficking of a child from the Roma community, from which potential victims are especially vulnerable. The investigation, initiated in March 2010, included some government officials. Citing a lack of credible evidence, the state prosecutor determined the individuals under investigation could not be prosecuted for trafficking. Available at http://www.state.gov/documents/organization/164453.pdf.

29.   Editorial by Vinko Dumancic, the director of the BiH Border Police for EUPM *Mission Mag* #74 on 14 June 2010. Available at http://www.eupm.org/FCKeditor/Images/Media/Mission percent20Mag/MissionMag percent20074.pdf.

30.   Data extracted from table 7.4 of the UNDP's Early Warning Report 2010.

31.   Interview with an EUPM officer in April 2006.

32.   "The Civilian Planning and Conduct Capability (CPCC) is the permanent structure responsible for an autonomous operational conduct of civilian ESDP operations. Under the political control and strategic direction of the Political and Security Committee and the overall authority of the High Representative, the CPCC ensures the effective planning and conduct of civilian ESDP crisis management operations, as well as the proper implementation of all mission-related tasks." More available at http://consilium.europa.eu/eeas/security-defence/csdp-structures-and-instruments/cpcc.aspx?lang=en.

33.   UNDP's early warning report 2010 table 1.10.

34.   The text of the Strategic Agreement between the EUROPOL and BiH is available at https://www.europol.europa.eu/sites/default/files/flags/bosniaherzegovia.pdf.

35.   Available at http://www.europol.europa.eu/Docs/PrioritiesofEuropolinWesternBalkans01April2009.pdf .

36.   The mandate of the EUSR is available at the official website at http://www.eusrbih.eu/gen-info/?cid=2000,1,1.

37.   Ibid.

38.   For the mandate of the OHR, Annex 10 of the DPA, please see http://www.ohr.int/ohr-info/gen-info/default.asp?content_id=38612.

39.   Available at http://www.eusrbih.eu/gen-info/?cid=283,1,1.

SIX

Conclusion

The European Union (EU) is not an effective actor for peace in Bosnia-Herzegovina (BiH). There are a number of factors contributing to this ineffectiveness. First, the European Union institutions are not equipped to engage in a postconflict applicant country. Second, the EU's actions toward BiH are built on a preconceived moral superiority and self-righteousness that causes rigidity in its policy making. Third, there is no unity of action among the EU members. The leading members of the European Union, Germany, France, and the United Kingdom, develop their separate foreign policy agendas on the issue of expansion. And, as a fourth factor, due to expansion fatigue among the European Union citizens, especially during the prolonged economic crisis, the EU leaders are not able to pronounce any clear accession date for Bosnia-Herzegovina without BiH demonstrating any concrete achievements in its reform process.

FACTOR 1. EUROPEAN UNION INSTITUTIONS ARE NOT EQUIPPED TO ENGAGE IN A POSTCONFLICT APPLICANT COUNTRY

The institutions of the European Union are designed to deal with applicant countries that have functional state bureaucracies. So are the EU policies that are formulated on a false premise that any applicant country has a working government by default. The EU accession is essentially an adaptation of a long and complex set of bureaucratic, procedural changes. To join the EU, an applicant country must meet the EU standards on political freedoms and economic development. All applicant countries must fulfill the Copenhagen criteria and complete the adoption of the thirty-five chapters of the Acquis Communautaire.[1]

The Copenhagen criteria, established in June 1993 by the European Council in Copenhagen, entail a candidate country to have:

- stable institutions that guarantee democracy, the rule of law, human rights, and respect for and protection of minorities;
- a functioning market economy, as well as the ability to cope with the pressure of competition and the market forces at work in the Union;
- the ability to assume the obligations of membership, in adherence to the objectives of political, economic, and monetary union.[2]

Once an applicant country is elevated to the status of a candidate then it has to adopt the chapters of the Acquis Communautaire to qualify as a full member of the EU. Completion of the Acquis means that the applicant country is ready to assume the political and financial commitments required as a member of the EU club, including the monetary union. The accession is a long process for many applicant countries that already have effective state bodies; challenges are much greater for those applicant countries that are postconflict societies at the same time.

Many postconflict societies are defined by political authoritarianism, endemic corruption, and lack of effective state institutions (Collier and Hoeffler 2004). Bosnia-Herzegovina is not exempt from this characterization. Most of the politicians in BiH, fifteen years after the war ended, still speak an authoritarian language. Public perceptions of corruption run especially high. Moreover, most of the state-level institutions remain defunct as the power-sharing structure of the Dayton Peace Agreement runs into hurdles between three constituent nations of Bosniaks, Serbs, and Croats. As we have discussed in chapter 2, the consociational system of BiH is designed to work only through the goodwill of the entity politicians. The checks and balances created by the Dayton constitution set up the state-level bodies as platforms of cooperation, rather than bodies that provide services.

The EU officials in charge of overseeing the accession process of BiH are frustrated. They have no counterpart at the BiH state level that is able to deliver any of the reforms in the European Partnership document. The deteriorating relations between the entities since 2006 makes the adoption of the reforms harder. Strikingly, the frustration of the EU has not been translated into a search for alternative ways of engaging with the existing political system in Bosnia. The EU accession perspective is not able to generate political will for the reforms that call for strong state institutions. The push for the centralization of power only serves to reinforce the pro-independence political trajectory in Republika Srpska. The alternative to the current stigma would be conducting the accession negotiations separately with each entity. This is a politically risky alternative considering that two-track accession talks might mean the end of the sovereign state of Bosnia-Herzegovina. But it is time for EU officials to consider the viability of this option. A two-track negotiation process could be more successful with a clause saying that none of the entities would be allowed into the EU without the others completing the process and thus joining the EU as Bosnia-Herzegovina. Making this decision would require a degree of decisiveness and clarity that is unobserved in the risk-averse culture of the European Union institutions.

FACTOR 2: THE EU POLICIES TOWARD BIH ARE BUILT ON A PRECONCEIVED SENSE OF MORAL SUPERIORITY AND SELF-RIGHTEOUSNESS

The EU is a normative power. On many occasions, EU politicians express their commitments to placing universal norms and principles at the heart of EU's relations with its member states and the world (Manners 2005). The EU institutional culture presumes that applicant countries go through a normative transformation via fulfilling the Copenhagen criteria and the full adoption of the Acquis. An EU member is expected to share the same values with the rest of the members. The European Union accession a political modernization blueprint. Applicant countries embrace the model by adopting its rules and procedures and surrender a part of their autonomy in exchange for effectiveness and stability. The former candidate countries of the 2004 enlargement, most of which were former authoritarian Warsaw bloc countries, willingly adopted the rules and regulations of the EU Acquis and the Copenhagen Criteria that have transformed them into fully functioning liberal democracies. Such a fast-paced democratic transition at such a large scale, according to pro-European scholars, confirmed the European Union's position in the world as a normative power.

The EU relentlessly reminds Bosnian politicians of their duty to carry out these reforms in the European Partnership document. According to the EU Commission it is the responsibility of Bosnia-Herzegovina as an applicant country to legislate and implement the reforms. If BiH fails to deliver, the EU bears no responsibility. The EU institutions are not designed to reflect on the effectiveness of their policies. The impact assessment tools in place focus on the short-term outcomes and outputs outlined in the annual progress reports. BiH authorities are criticized about their stagnation on different reform areas identified in the European Partnership document and applauded in rare cases of progress. The EU officials firmly believe that the EU should not be fabricating political will for BiH where there is none. EU's attitude indicates a sense of self-righteousness built on the positive experience with the Central and Eastern European countries. All Central and Eastern European countries successfully completed their accession processes without much difficulty; the capacity of the state institutions in these countries helped them adopt the acquis quite successfully.

BiH's failure to move forward in the accession process is not necessarily the result of lack of commitment to democratize by Bosnian politicians. It is the result of the RS political elite's opposition to strengthen the capacity of the state-level institutions at the expense of the entities. There is a high level support for EU membership among the Bosnians, but accession through strengthening state-level institutions is not the way out. EU fails to recognize that its persistence in pushing for capacity-building reforms at the state level will not deliver sustainable results. Its sense of self-righteousness causes institutional blindness and rigidity in its policy making. As Bosnia stagnates and falls behind its neighbors in the EU integration process, EU prefers to monitor and draft negative annual progress reports.

FACTOR 3: THERE IS NO UNITY OF ACTION AMONG THE EU MEMBERS

Contrary to the official line, the European Union institutions and the EU member states often contradict each other in Bosnia-Herzegovina. Member states have the advantage of leveraging their diplomatic services and development agencies more quickly and efficiently than the EU community and council instruments. Representatives of some of the EU members sitting on the Steering Board of the Peace Implementation Council, the international body responsible for overseeing the full implementation of the Dayton Peace Agreement, send contradictory messages to Bosnian politicians. Such noise diminishes the leverage of the European Union over the Bosnian politicians as a whole.

Bosnian politicians are well aware of the fact that the real decision makers at the EU are the heads of the EU member states, not the EU bureaucrats. If Bosnian politicians play their cards right with the leading EU members, they know they can move forward with the accession process without any real implementation of reforms. Many times amid the pressure from the member states the European Union upgraded the association status of Bosnia-Herzegovina. The EU has been keen to see the occasional memoranda of understanding between Bosniak, Croat, and Serb politicians on the reform agenda as a sign of commitment to the EU accession process. The case of police reform discussed is a clear example to the noise. For a long time, the European Union has been uncompromising on the unification of the Federation and RS police forces. However, some EU members were alarmed when Republika Srpska politicians turned the debate on police reform into one on the future viability of Bosnia-Herzegovina as a country. Therefore, once the Bosniak and Serbian politicians agreed to speak on possible options for police reform, the EU softened its stance and initiated the Stabilization and Association Agreement (SAA). The EU had to settle for less. The police reform still remains incomplete. The European Union's credibility as a serious political player is severely damaged. It became obvious to Bosnian politicians that the European Union can be manipulated by confrontational political discourse.

FACTOR 4: THE EU IS NOT ABLE TO PRONOUNCE ANY CLEAR ACCESSION DATE FOR BOSNIA-HERZEGOVINA

The expansion fatigue of the European Union is expected to persist after the global financial crisis shook the economies of individual EU member states and weakened the prestige of the Euro as a reserve currency. The recent financial meltdown cast doubts on the viability of the European common market. Politically and financially, the European Union is not in a place to absorb a new wave of enlargement. The EU is hardly consolidating the Eurozone economies in the wake of the Greek bailout and financial crises in Italy, Spain, Portugal, and Ireland.

Public opinion in the EU members is opposed to a further enlargement, bearing in mind the additional financial burden will be on their shoulders as EU taxpayers.[3] The completion of the 2004 eastern enlargement with ten new member states, required reform in the European Union institutions and restructuring of the relations between the member states and Brussels. However, by the summer of 2005, public opinion in many EU countries turned against further consolidation of the Union. The "no" votes by the French and the Dutch to the proposed EU constitution have ended the euphoria prevalent during the preceding decade. Bosnian politicians are well aware of this fatigue and do not see the EU integration option as a possibility in the near future. Picking up the EU flag is not considered as a viable political alternative in Bosnian politics. Instead, Bosnian politicians continue forging alliances within their own ethnic communities and prefer to engage in daily verbal assaults against politicians of other ethnic groups. This is also true for the rest of the Western Balkans and Turkey with the exception of Croatia, which is set to join the Union by 2013. The global financial crisis shifted the attention of Germany, France, and the UK to restructuring their economies toward more conservative, protectionist models. The largely negative European public opinion[4] could get worse as unemployment rates continue to grow. The arrival of a cheaper workforce from the Western Balkans could be seen as a threat.

The overall strategy for the Western Balkans enlargement is not clear yet. There are two prevailing views on the matter. One is to evaluate each applicant Western Balkan country on its individual performance. The second view is to accept all of the Western Balkan countries together regardless of their individual achievements, in order not to cause additional inequalities in the region. For all the reasons above, EU is not able to pronounce any definite date of accession for Bosnia-Herzegovina. In Bosnia-Herzegovina politicians de-evaluated the priority of the EU integration on the list of things to do. The lack of a comprehensive strategy and date of accession undermine the political leverage of the European Union.

CONCLUSION

This book analyzed Bosnia-Herzegovina's current political challenges, looked into the effectiveness of the European Union accession perspective and provided an overview of the EU's crisis management competencies at play in BiH. The EU integration is a tool that is underutilized and mismanaged in BiH. The EU's effectiveness in BiH as a peace actor is conditioned by the speed at which BiH transforms its political institutions, processes, and culture into a working liberal democracy.

The main political challenge of Bosnia-Herzegovina is its dysfunctional Dayton system. The Dayton Agreement set up a complicated consociational system that grants extensive executive powers to the entity politicians. The country has four levels of governance, where a fragile balance in ethnic representation is set up among three constituent nations. Making and implementing a political decision requires a number of balancing acts between the entities and their representatives at the state level. The Dayton system is designed to work only through the goodwill of Bosnian politicians. There is not a clear mechanism of checks and balances that would keep the country running in the common occasions of contention between politicians. The representative body of the international community, the OHR, has a nondemocratic mandate that allows for intervention in political situations that are considered harmful for the full implementation of the Dayton Peace Agreement. In the past fifteen years, some of the High Representatives used their nondemocratic mandates without much hesitation to remove elected politicians from office. Such discrete measures by the international community have curtailed the consolidation of Bosnian democracy and created a new class of reactionary politicians in the Republika Srpska who create their political turf through their opposition to the international community and the EU reforms. As the RS politicians harden their positions, politicians in the Federation adopt a similar confrontational language against the RS that blocks any possibility of cooperation between the two entities on the EU reforms, in some cases prompting the intervention of the international community to break the deadlock. Bosnia does not perform exceptionally well on the economic front either. The unemployment rate among youth is high; there is a widely shared perception of corruption in all segments of the society and government in a youth that is extremely pessimistic about the future of

the country. Given the bleak economic outlook, the European Union integration is advertised by the international community as the only way out.

The future European Union membership can be the way out for BiH.
The pull of the EU membership perspective can replace the push of the
international community. However, the EU's strategy in the country does
not take into account Bosnia's political dilemma, torn between the desire
to normalize and the concern to preserve the Dayton system. With the
dysfunctional Dayton system in place, BiH government lacks the capacity
to negotiate the thirty-five chapters of the EU acquis. EU has recognized
this discrepancy and developed a European Partnership model where
BiH is tasked to implement a list of capacity-building reforms on the
short, medium, and long term until its accession to the EU. The Stabilization and Association Process (SAP) serves as the core tool of this process.
Nonetheless, more than a year after the signing of the Stabilization and
Association Agreement (SAA) Bosnia has not managed to make any significant progress on the reforms. The EU failed to recognize that the
reform proposals for stronger state institutions further polarize the Bosnian politics. Unless the European Union considers a two-track approach
that would negotiate the integration process with the entities, Bosnia-
Herzegovina's membership in the EU will remain as an aspiration.

The EU has taken over the policing and peacekeeping missions from
the international community over the past decade in order to assess its
military and civilian crisis management competencies in the relatively
calm and secure environment of Bosnia. The EU Police Mission has
evolved over the years and become an effective programmatic mission
that provides on-site mentoring for the Bosnian police to battle against
corruption and transnational criminal networks that use the porous borders of the country for human and drug smuggling. The EUFOR-Althea
mission has not been tested as a peacekeeping mission with any outstanding security challenge so far and is gradually phasing out of Bosnia.
The EUFOR achieved a daily working experience that is rolled out to
other military crisis missions. The newly enforced European Union Special Representative (EUSR) is a rather belated initiative that could integrate the community and crisis management competencies of the EU. It is
early to assess the performance of the EUSR, but it is essential for the
EUSR to support the EU as a relevant actor in Bosnian politics as the EU
sinks deeper into economic crisis.

FINAL WORDS

The Dayton Peace Agreement has set up a consociational order to allow for a balanced representation of ethnicities on all levels of governance. The Dayton Constitution provided optimal guarantees to the conflict parties that preserved the territorial integrity of Bosnia while giving broad political autonomy to Republika Srpska. In the past fifteen years, Bosnia-Herzegovina has slowly recovered from the physical damage caused by the war. The international community has played a key role in this recovery by assisting the Bosnians to rebuild their social and economic infrastructure. During this period, the two entities developed their own political systems, gradually moving further apart from each other amid the pressure from the international community to centralize the country. The society and politics remain fragmented along ethnic lines more than ever.

Despite its political setbacks and uncertainties, Bosnia-Herzegovina wants to become a member of the European Union along with its neighbors in the Western Balkans. The European Union has an opportunity in Bosnia to prove that the EU membership perspective could transform a dysfunctional postconflict, multiethnic society into one that generates wealth and security for its citizens regardless of ethnic backgrounds. The EU has failed to meet these expectations so far. The EU strategy misinterprets the Dayton System and tries to resolve the governance deficit at the state level. As a result, almost all reform initiatives focused on building the capacity of state-level institutions backfired due to inter-ethnic political warfare among Bosnian politicians.

There is a growing concern among the international community that Bosnia will never complete its obligations and will remain as an underdeveloped society on the fringes of the EU. It is time the European Union takes control and designs a new two-track integration strategy for BiH that would allow entities to negotiate with the EU separately, but at the same time guarantee that they join the EU together as Bosnia-Herzegovina. The real strength of the EU has been the innovativeness of its founders to bring sustainable peace to the European continent after an extraordinarily destructive world war. Bringing sustainable peace to Bosnia requires flexibility and innovativeness; EU has these necessary resources to tap into.

NOTES

1. Any country seeking membership in the European Union (EU) must conform to the conditions set out by Article 49 and the principles laid down in Article 6(1) of the Treaty on European Union. Relevant criteria were established by the Copenhagen European Council in 1993 and strengthened by the Madrid European Council in 1995.

2. Conclusions of the Presidency of the Council of European Union in Copenhagen on June 21–22, 1993 are available at http://europa.eu/rapid/pressReleasesAction.do?reference=DOC/93/3&format=HTML&aged=1&language=EN&guiLanguage=en.

3. According to the Standard Eurobarometer Autumn 2010 Report #7, 4 the support for BiH's accession into the EU is at a low 35 percent; similarly, the figures that indicate the EU public opinion support for the future accession of the other Western Balkan countries run very low, Serbia 34 percent, Albania and Kosovo 29 percent, Macedonia 35 percent, and Montenegro 36 percent. Croatia, which is set to join the EU by 2013, receive a 47 percent approval of the EU public opinion for its accession. Results are available at http://ec.europa.eu/public_opinion/archives/eb/eb74/eb74_publ_en.pdf.

4. "Fewer than half of Europeans are in favor of further enlargement of the European Union to include other countries in future years (47 percent, i.e., 1 percentage point more than in autumn 2007), compared with four out of ten who oppose the idea (39 percent)." Results of the Eurobarometer Survey #69 "The European Union Today and Tomorrow " conducted between March and May 2008 and published in November 2008, available at http://ec.europa.eu/public_opinion/archives/eb/eb69/eb69_part3_en.pdf

Bibliography

Arendt, Hannah. "On Violence," in *Crises of the Republic*. Orlando, FL: Harcourt. Brace & Co., 1972.

Aristotle. *The Politics, revised edition*. New York: Penguin, 1983.

Barker, Ernest. *Reflections on Government*. London: Oxford University Press, 1942.

Basch, Raymond M. "The Effects of Ethnic Separation on Democratization: A Comparative Study." *East European Quarterly* 32 (1998): 221–237.

Bertelsmann Stiftung. *BTI 2010—Bosnia and Herzegovina Country Report*. Gütersloh: Bertelsmann Stiftung, 2009.

Bieber, Florian. "Muslim Identity in the Balkans before the Establishment of Nation States." *Nationalities Papers* 28 (2000): 13–28.

Bideleux, Robert and Ian Jeffries. *The Balkans: A Post-Communist History*. London: Routledge, 2007.

Bougarel, Xavier. *Bosnie: Anatomie d'un Conflit*. Paris: La Découverte, 1996.

Bringa, Tone. *Being Muslim the Bosnian Way: Identity and Community in a Central Bosnian Village*. Princeton: Princeton University, 1995.

Brioni Declaration. Brioni, Croatia, July 18, 1991.

Brown, Steven David. *Combating International Crime: The Longer Arm of the Law*. London: Routledge-Cavendish, 2008

Carpenter, Ted G. "Jackboot Nation Building: The West Brings 'Democracy' to Bosnia." *Mediterranean Quarterly* 11, no. 2 (2000): 1–22.

Castells, Manuel. *The Rise of the Network Society, The Information Age: Economy, Society and Culture Vol. I. 2nd Edition*. Cambridge, MA: Blackwell, 2000.

Civil Society Promotion Center in Sarajevo.Environment in Bosnia-Herzegovina. Sarajevo, 2002. http://enrin.grida.no/htmls/bosnia/bosnia2002/index.html.

Collier, Paul and Anke Hoeffler. "Greed and Grievance in Civil War." *Oxford Economic Papers* 56 (2004): 563–595.

Council of the European Union. General Affairs Council Meeting Conclusions. Brussels, April 29, 1997.

———. *Summary Note on the Joint Report by Javier Solana, EU High Representative for the CFSP, and Olli Rehn, EU Commissioner for Enlargement, on a Reinforced EU Presence in Bosnia and Herzegovina*. Brussels, October 17, 2006.

Council of the European Union. Presidency Conclusions. Copenhagen, June 22–23, 1993.

———. Presidency Conclusions. Madrid, December 15–16, 1995.

———. *Presidency Conclusions*. Vienna, December 11–12, 1998.

———. *Presidency Conclusions*. Santa Maria de Feira, June 19–20, 2000.

Council of the European Union. *Declaration of the Zagreb Summit*. Zagreb, November 24, 2000.

Council of the European Union. *Council Regulation on the Establishment of Partnerships in the Framework of the Stabilisation and Association Process*. Brussels, March 22, 2004.

Crick, Bernard. *In Defense of Politics*. Baltimore, MD: Penguin, 1964.

Cutright, Philips. "National Political Development: Measurement and Analysis." *American Sociological Review* 28 (1963): 253–264.

Dahl, Robert A. *Polyarchy , Participation and Opposition*. New Haven: Yale University Press, 1971.

Dahrendorf, Ralf. *Class and Class Conflict in Industrial Society*. Stanford, CA: Stanford University Press, 1959.

Diez, Thomas. "Constructing the Self and Changing Others: Reconsidering 'Normative Power Europe." *Millennium - Journal of International Studies* 33 (2005): 613–636.

Dowley, Kathleen and Brian Silver."Social Capital, Ethnicity, and Support for Democracy in the Post-Communist States." *Europe/Asia Studies* 54 (2002): 505–527.

Dumancic, Vinko." Editorial." *EUPM MissionMag* 74 (2010).

EU Inter-Governmental Conference.

EU-NATO Declaration on ESDP. Brussels, December 16, 2002.

EU-Western Balkans Summit Conclusions. Thessaloniki, June 21, 2003.

European Commission for Democracy through Law (Venice Commission). *Opinion on the Constitutional Situation in Bosnia and Herzegovina and the Powers of the High Representative adopted by the Venice Commission at its 62nd plenary session (Venice, 11–12 March 2005)*. Venice, March 11, 2005

———. *Report from the Commission to the Council on the preparedness of Bosnia and Herzegovina to negotiate a Stabilisation and Association Agreement with the European Union*. Brussels, 2003.

———. *Opinion on Different Proposals for the Election of the Presidency of Bosnia and Herzegovina endorsed by the Commission at its 66th plenary session (Venice, 17–18 March 2006), Opinion no. 374/2006*. Strasbourg, March 20, 2006.

European Council Declaration on Strengthening the Common European Policy on Security and Defense. Conclusions of the Presidency of the European Council. Cologne, June 3–4, 1999.

European Union Council Meeting Conclusions. Brussels, February 26, 1997.

Forster, Anthony and William Wallace. "Common Foreign Security Policy." In *Policy-Making in the European Union* edited by Helen Wallace and William Wallace. Oxford: Oxford University Press, 2000: 481–485.

Franco-British Summit Joint Declaration on European Defense. Saint-Malo, 4 December 1998.

Freedom House. *Freedom in the World 2011 Survey*. Washington, DC, 2011. http://www.freedomhouse.org/images/File/fiw/historical/ElectoralDemocracyNumbers-FIW1989–2011.pdf.

Foreign Policy Initiative BH (VPI). "The Myth about the Closure of OHR." *Policy Analysis* 4 (2011).

Friedrich, Carl J. *Constitutional Government and Democracy: Theory and Practice in Europe and America*. Boston: Little, Brown and Company, 1942.

Friis, Lykke and Anna Murphy. "Turbo-Charged Negotiations: The EU and the Stability Pact for South Eastern Europe." *Journal of European Public Policy* 7 (2000): 767–786.

Fukuyama, Francis. *The End of History and the Last Man*. New York: Free Press, 1992.

Furnivall, John Sydenham. *Colonial Policy and Practice: A Comparative Study of Burma and Netherlands India*. New York: New York University Press, 1956.

General Framework Agreement for Peace, Annex IV, Constitution of Bosnia and Herzegovina, 1995. http://www.ccbh.ba/public/down/US-TAV_BOSNE_I_HERCEGOVINE_engl.pdf

Gherghisan, Mihaela. "European Defence Agreement Reached." *EU Observer* 12 December 2003.

Gnesotto, Nicole. *EU Security and Defense Policy: The First Five Years (1999–2004)*. Paris: Institute for Security Studies, 2004.

Haine , Jean-Yves. "From Laeken to Copenhagen. European defense: Core Documents III." *EU-ISS—Chaillot Paper*, No. 57 (2003).

The ICG report on "Bosnia's Stalled Police Reform: No Progress, No EU" dated September 6, 2005.

Institute for War and Peace Reporting, Impact of the Bosnian War on the Media, Institute for War and Peace Reporting 1996 June.

International Crisis Group, "Policing the Police in Bosnia: A Further Reform Agenda," *Europe Report* No. 130, May 10, 2002

———. "Bosnia's Nationalist Governments: Paddy Ashdown and the Paradoxes of State Building." Balkans Report No. 146. Sarajevo, Brussels: ICG, July 22, 2003. http://www.crisisgroup.org/~/media/Files/europe/Bosnia%20146.pdf.

———. "Bosnia's Stalled Police Reform: No Progress, No EU." *Europe Report* No. 164. Sarajevo, Brussels, September 6, 2005.

International Press Institute-South East Europe Media Organization (SEEMO). *2004 World Press Freedom Review, Bosnia-Herzegovina Report*. Sarajevo, 2004.

International Tribunal for the Prosecution of Persons Responsible for Serious Violations of International Humanitarian Law Committed in the Territory of Former Yugoslavia since 1991. *Sentencing Judgement on the Case of Prosecutor V. Biljana Plavšić*. The Hague, February 27, 2003. http://www.icty.org/x/cases/plavsic/tjug/en/pla-tj030227e.pdf.

Interview with Raffi Gregorian, the-then Head of the NATO Contingency in the Defense Ministry of BiH, Sarajevo, June 14, 2006.

Interview with official from the US Embassy in Sarajevo on June 13, 2006.

Jefferson, Thomas. *Letter to James Madison, Federalist Papers*. Washington, DC: Library of Congress, 1789.

Jelacic, Nerma, Mustajbegovic, Saida and Gordana Katana, "Poll Upset for Big Three in Bosnia" *Balkan Insight*, October 5, 2006. http://old.balkaninsight.com/en/main/analysis/5202/?tpl.

Kagan, Robert. "Power and Weakness." *Policy Review* 113 (200 2).

Knaus, Gerald and Felix Martin. "Travails of the European Raj." *Journal of Democracy* 14 (2003): 60–74.

Kutnjak Ivković, Sanja, and Tara O'Connor Shelley. "The Bosnian Police and Police Integrity: A Continuing Story." *European Journal of Criminology* 2 (2005): 428–464.

Lehmbruch, Gerhard. "A Non-Competitive Pattern of Conflict Management in Liberal Democracy: The Case of Switzerland, Austria and Lebanon." *Paper presented at the Seventh World Congress of the International Political Science Association, Brussels, 1967.*

Lerner, Daniel. *The Passing of Traditional Society: Modernizing the Middle East*. Glencoe, IL: Free Press, 1958.

Levi, Michael. "The Organization of Serious Crime." In *The Oxford Handbook of Criminology, Third Edition* edited by Mike Maguire, Rod Morgan, and Robert Reiner. Oxford: Oxford University Press, 2002.

Lexau, Skjold. Bosnia Herzegovina: Office of the High Representative 2003–2004. *NORDEM Report* 16 (2004).

Lijphart, Arend. *The Politics of Accommodation: Pluralism and Democracy in the Netherlands*. Berkeley: University of California Press, 1968.

———. "Consociational Democracy." *World Politics* 21 (1969): 207–225.

———. *Democracy in plural societies: A comparative exploration.* New Haven: Yale University Press, 1977.

———. *Patterns of Democracy: Government Forms and Performance in Thirty-Six Countries.* New Haven, CT: Yale University Press, 1999.

Lipset, Seymour Martin. *Political Man: The Social Bases of Politics.* Garden City, NY: Doubleday and Company, 1960.

Lorwin, Val Rogin. "Segmented Pluralism: Ideological Cleavages and Political Cohesion in the Smaller European Democracies." *Comparative Politics* 3 (1971): 141–175.

Madrid European Council Presidency Conclusions. Madrid, 15 And 16 December 1995.

Major, Claudia and Christian Molling. "EU Battlegroups: What Contribution to European Defense? Progress and Prospects of European Rapid Response Forces." *Stiftung Wissenschaft und Politik Research Paper* 8 (2011).

Malcolm, Noel. Bosnia, *A Short History.* Macmillan, London, 1996.

Maljević, Almir, Datzer, Darko, Muratbegović, Elmedin and Muhamed Budimli ć. *Overtly about Police Corruption.* Sarajevo: Association of Criminalists in Bosnia and Herzegovina, 2006.

Manners, Ian. "The Constitutive Nature of Values, Images and Principles in the European Union." In *Values and Principles in European Union Foreign Policy,* edited by Sonia Lucarelli and Ian Manners. London: Routledge,2005.

———. "Normative Power Europe Reconsidered: Beyond the Crossroads." *Journal of European Public Policy* 13 (2006): 182–199

McClosky, Herbert. "Consensus and Ideology in American Politics." *American Political Science Review* 58 (1964): 361–382

Merlingen, Michael, and Rasa Ostrauskaite. "The Implementation of the ESDP. Issues and Tentative Generalizations." In *European Security and Defense Polic: An Implementation Perspective,* edited by Michael Merlingen with Rasa Ostrauskaite, 188–205. London: Routledge, 2008.

Mill, John Stuart. Considerations on Representative Government. New York: The Liberal Arts Press, 1958 [1861].

Monaco, Annalisa. "Operation Concordia and Berlin Plus: NATO and the EU Take Stock." *NATO Notes* 5 (2003): 9–11.

Moore, Barrington Jr. *Social origins of dictatorship and democracy: Lord and peasant in the making of the modern world.* Boston: Beacon Press, 1966.

Mostar Declaration on Honouring the Commitments for Implementation of the Police Reform with Aim to Initial and Sign the Stabilisation and Association Agreement. Mostar, October 28, 2007.

Nye, Joseph S. *Soft Power: The Means to Success in World Politics.* New York: Public Affairs, 2004.

O'Donnel, Guillermo, and Phillipe C. Schmitter. "Transitions from Authoritarian Rule: Tentative Conclusions about Uncertain Democracies." In Transitions from Authoritarian Rule: Comparative Perspectives , edited by Guillermo O'Donnell, Phillipe.C. Schmitter and Laurence Whitehead. Baltimore: The Johns Hopkins University Press, 1986.

Office of the High Representative (OHR). *14th Report by the High Representative for Implementation of the Peace Agreement to the Secretary-General of the United Nations.* Sarajevo, July 16, 1999.

————. *Decision Removing Ante Jelavic from His Position as the Croat Member of the BiH Presidency.* Sarajevo, March 7, 2001.

————. *Agreement of the Implementation of the Constituent People's Decision of the Constitutional Court of Bosnia-Herzegovina.* Sarajevo, March 27, 2002.

————. *Decision Suspending All Judicial and Prosecutorial Appointments in BiH (Except to the Bih and the Entity Constitutional Courts, the BiH Human Rights Chamber, the Bih Court, and All Courts in the Brcko District) Pending the Restructuring of the Judicial System.* Sarajevo, April 4, 2002.

————. *Address by the High Representative, Christian Schwarz-Schilling to the Permanent Council of the OSCE.* Vienna, March 16, 2006.

————. "Towards Ownership: From Peace Implementation to Euro-Atlantic Integration." *Communique by the PIC Steering Board.* Sarajevo, June 23, 2006.

————. "Maintaining Progress." *Communique by the PIC Steering Board.* Sarajevo, February 27, 2007.

————. *31st Report of the High Representative for Implementation of the Peace Agreement on Bosnia and Herzegovina to the Secretary-General of the United Nations.* Sarajevo, May 16, 2007.

————. *Decision to Remove Mr. Predrag Čeranić from his Current Position in the Intelligence and Security Agency of Bosnia and Herzegovina.* Sarajevo, May 30, 2008.

Office of the United States Special Representative in Europe, Treaty Establishing the European Defense Community. As the Text Contained in Sen. Exec. Doc. No. Q and R, 82d Cong., 2d Sess. (1952), 167–251.

OSCE Office For Democratic Institutions and Human Rights (ODIHR). *Final Report on Bosnia and Herzegovina Elections, 12–13 September 1998.* Warsaw, 1999. http://www.osce.org/odihr/elections/bih/14045.

————. *Final Report on Bosnia and Herzegovina General Elections, 5 October 2002.* Warsaw, 2003. http://www.osce.org/odihr/elections/bih/14001.

————. *Final Report on Bosnia and Herzegovina General Elections, 1 October 2006.* Warsaw, 2007. http://www.osce.org/odihr/elections/bih/23945.

Palmer, L. K. " Police reforms in Bosnia-Herzegovina: External pressure and internal resistance." In *Transforming the Police in Eastern and Central Europe* edited by Marina Caparini and Otwin Marenin Műnster, Germany: LIT Verlag/Transaction Publishers, 2004.

Peace Implementation Council (PIC). *Bonn Conclusions of the PIC Main Meeting.* Bonn, December 10, 1997.

Pickering, Paula M. "Generating Social Capital for Bridging Ethnic Divisions in the Balkans: Case Studies of Two Bosniak Cities." *Ethnic and Racial Studies* 29 (2006): 79–103.

Portes, Alejandro. "Social Capital: Its Origins and Applications in Modern Sociology." *Annual Review of Sociology* 24 (1998): 1–24.

Pugh, Michael. "Introduction: The ownership of regeneration and peacebuilding." In *Regeneration of War-Torn Societies* edited by Michael Pugh. New York: St. Martin's Press, 2004.

Putnam, Robert D. *Making Democracy Work: Civic Traditions in Modern Italy.* Princeton: Princeton University Press, 1993.

———. *The Collapse and Revival of American Community*. New York: Simon & Schuster, 2000.

———. "Democracy, Development, and the Civic Community: Evidence from an Italian Experiment." In *Culture and Development in Africa: Proceedings of an International Conference Held at the World Bank, Washington, D.C., April 2 and 3, 1992* edited by Ismail Serageldin and June Taboroff , 29–76. Washington, DC: The World Bank, 1992.

Quille, Gerrard and Joceyln Mawdsley. "Equipping the Rapid Reaction Force: Options for and Constraints on a European Defense Equipment Strategy." *Bonn International Centre for Conversion (BICC) Paper* 33 (2003): 29–30.

Republic of Srpska Investment Development Bank. *Economic Monitor No. 7*. Banja Luka, 2011.

Ranson, Jenny. *International Intervention in Media, The Open Broadcast Network: A Case Study in Bosnia and Herzegovina*. Geneva: Institute for Peace, Media and Security, University of Peace, 2005.

Reynié, Dominique. *Victory for the Nationalists in the Presidential and General Elections in Bosnia-Herzegovina: Results of the General Elections of 5th October 2002*. Paris:Fondation Robert Schumann, European Elections Monitor, 2002. http://www.robert-schuman.eu/oee.php?num=34.

The Rome Declaration on October 1984.

Ruma, Inan Sadan. "The Role of the International Community in Democratization in Bosnia-Herzegovina." PhD diss., Ankara: Middle East Technical University, 2008.

Rustow, Dankwart. A. "Transitions to Democracy: Toward a Dynamic Model." *Comparative Politics* 2 (1970): 337–363.

Sampson, Steven. "Beyond Transition: Rethinking Elite Configurations in the Balkans." In *Postsocialism: Ideals, Ideologies and Practices in Eurasia*, edited by Chris M. Hann, 297–316. London: Routledge, 2002.

Santa Maria Da Feira European Council Conclusions of the Presidency held on 19–20 June 2000.

Schattschneider, Elmer Eric. *The Semi-Sovereign People: A Realist's View of Democracy in America*. New York: Holt, Rinehart and Winston, 1960.

Shils , Edward Albert. *The Virtue of Civility: Selected Essays on Liberalism, Tradition, and Civil Society*. Indianapolis: Liberty Fund, 1997.

Sebastian, Sofia. *Assessing Democracy Assistance: Bosnia*, FRIDE Report 2010.

Solioz, Christoph, and Svebor Dizdarevic. *Ownership Process in Bosnia and Herzegovina*. Baden-Baden: Nomos, 2003.

The Speech of the NATO Secretary General, Jaap de Hoop Scheffer, at the Signing of the Partnership for Peace (PfP) Agreement with Bosnia and Herzegovina. December 14, 2006.

Standard Eurobarometer Autumn 2010 Report #7. http://ec.europa.eu/public_opinion/archives/eb/eb74/eb74_publ_en.pdf.

Tönnies, Ferdinand. *Gemeinschaft und Gesellschaft: Grundbegriffen der Reinen Soziologie. 8th Edition*. Darmstadt: Wissenschaftliche Buchgesellschaft, 1935.

Treaty Establishing the Western European Union (WEU), Paris, October 23, 1954.

Treaty of Amsterdam Amending the Treaty on European Union, the Treaties Establishing the European Communities and Certain Related Acts, October 2, 1997.

Treaty of Economic, Social and Cultural Collaboration and Collective Self-Defense, Brussels, March 17, 1948.

Treaty of Lisbon amending the Treaty on European Union and the Treaty establishing the European Community, signed at Lisbon, December 13, 2007.

Truman, David B. *The Governmental Process: Political Interests and Public Opinion.* New York: Alfred A. Knopf, 1951.

Tus, Anton. "The War up to the Sarajevo Ceasefire." In *The War in Croatia and Bosnia-Herzegovina 1991– 1995* edited by Branko Magaš and Ivo Žanić. London: Frank Cass Publishers, 2001.

UN Office on Drug and Crime (UNODC), *World Drug Report 2010* (United Nations Publication, Sales No. E.10.XI.13).

UN Security Council 3082nd Meeting Resolution 757. New York, May 30, 1992.

UN Security Council 3200th Meeting Resolution 820. New York, April 17, 1993.

UNDP. *Social Capital in Bosnia-Herzegovina: The Ties that Bind Sarajevo, 2009.* http://hdr.undp.org/en/reports/national/europethecis/bosniaherzegovina/Bosnia_NHDR_2009_EN.pdf.

UNDP. 2009 Early Warning Report on BiH. Sarajevo, 2010. http://www.undp.ba/upload/publications/Early%20Warning%20System%202009.pdf.

The United Nations Convention against Transnational Organized Crime, adopted by general assembly resolution 55/25 of November 15, 2000.

United Nations Development Programme (UNDP) Resident Representative office in Bosnia and Herzegovina. *Early Warning System 2010 Report on Bosnia and Herzegovina.* Sarajevo: United Nations Development Programme (UNDP) in Bosnia and Herzegovina, 2010.

United States Department of State, Bureau for International Narcotics and Law Enforcement Affairs. "Bosnia and Herzegovina." In *International Narcotics Control Strategy Report, Vol 1: Drug and Chemical Control,* 147–150. Washington, DC: US Department of State, 2011.

USAID. The 2009 NGO Sustainability Index for Central and Eastern Europe and Eurasia. Washington, DC, 2009.

Washington Treaty in 1949, thus of the North Atlantic Treaty Organization (NATO) http://www.usaid.gov/locations/europe_eurasia/dem_gov/ngoindex.

The World Bank Group. 2010 World Development Indicators (WDI). Washington, DC, 2011. http://data.worldbank.org/indicator.

Vaskovic, Slobodan. "Police Reform." *Patriot Magazine.* Banja Luka, May 9, 2005.

Wedel, Janine R. *Collision and Collusion: The Strange Case of Western Aid to Eastern Europe 1989–1998.* London: Macmillan, 1998.

Woodward, Susan L. *Balkan Tragedy: Chaos and Dissolution after the Cold War.* Washington, DC: Brookings Institution Press, 1995.

Index

About the Author

Doğa Ulaş Eralp is a scholar of international conflict, development, and democratization. He is the author of numerous articles and book chapters on the Western Balkans, Cyprus, the European Union, and Turkey. He also works extensively as a practitioner consulting international organizations and think tanks. He lives in Washington, DC.